Logic, Convention, and Common Knowledge

Logic, Convention, and Common Knowledge
A Conventionalist Account of Logic

Paul Syverson

CSLI PUBLICATIONS
Center for the Study of Language and Information
Stanford, California

Copyright © 2003
CSLI Publications
Center for the Study of Language and Information
Leland Stanford Junior University
Printed in the United States
07 06 05 04 03   5 4 3 2 1

Library of Congress Cataloging-in-Publication Data

Syverson, Paul
Logic, convention, and common knowledge :
a conventionalist account of logic / by Paul Syverson.
p.   cm.
(CSLI lectures notes ; no. 142)
Includes bibliographical references and index.
ISBN 1-57586-392-8 (pbk. : alk. paper)
ISBN 1-57586-391-X (hardback : alk. paper)
1. Logic. I. Title. II. Series.
BC71 .S98   2002
160–dc21   2002011452
CIP

∞ The acid-free paper used in this book meets the minimum requirements of the American National Standard for Information Sciences—Permanence of Paper for Printed Library Materials, ANSI Z39.48-1984.

CSLI was founded early in 1983 by researchers from Stanford University, SRI International, and Xerox PARC to further research and development of integrated theories of language, information, and computation. CSLI headquarters and CSLI Publications are located on the campus of Stanford University.

CSLI Publications reports new developments in the study of language, information, and computation. In addition to lecture notes, our publications include monographs, working papers, revised dissertations, and conference proceedings. Our aim is to make new results, ideas, and approaches available as quickly as possible. Please visit our web site at
http://cslipublications.stanford.edu/
for comments on this and other titles, as well as for changes and corrections by the author and publisher.

To James, Adlyn, Jennifer, Eleri, and James

Contents

Foreword   ix

Acknowledgments   xiii

1   Conventionalism: Setting Out the Problem   1

2   Games and Equilibria   11

3   Conventions   27

4   Common Knowledge and Coordination   37

5   Conventional Knowledge and Belief   49

6   The Origins of Mutual Understanding   65

7   A Logic of Familiarity   73

8   Three Grades of Epistemic Involvement   91

9   A Logic of Awareness   103

10   Convention Revisited   121

11   Conventions in Logic   133

References   149

Index   155

Foreword

Despite the impressive body of technical work that has taken place in mathematical logic over the last thirty years or so, little headway has been made in the philosophy of logic. We have still not made much progress in addressing the nature, scope, subject matter, and epistemology of logic. And it is still far from clear how to understand and adjudicate the claims of competing logical systems. But perhaps we can start the enterprise of answering these questions by providing an account of the nature of logic. For an account of what grounds the laws, truths, and properties of logic would presumably yield an understanding of the scope, subject matter, and epistemology of logic, and it would help clarify the competing claims of rival logics.

One view of logic that has appealed to many—though it has appalled some—is Conventionalism, the view that logical truths are true by convention. Conventionalism about logic has not, it must be said, been a terribly popular view of late, a fact which owes much to Quine's attack upon Carnap's Conventionalism in his *Truth by Convention*. Quine sees Conventionalism as facing a dilemma: either it is faced with postulating an infinite regress of conventions or it is explanatorily impotent. Many have accepted Quine's argument and concluded that Conventionalism about logic is philosophically bankrupt.[1]

In his *Logic, Convention, and Common Knowledge*, Paul Syverson develops an extremely impressive Conventionalist account of logic, which avoids infinite regresses while retaining explanatory potency. As such, Syverson provides an account of the nature of logic, which also sheds light upon the other philosophical issues surrounding logic. This

---

[1] There are, of course, exceptions. For an example of an interesting deflationary response to Quine's arguments, which accepts the explanatory impotence of Conventionalism but questions whether this is really a problem for Conventionalism, see Gary Ebbs's *Rule-Following and Realism*, Harvard University Press, 1997.

book consequently represents an important contribution to the philosophy of logic. But, as the following synopsis of its content reveals, it offers much more.

Any interesting brand of Conventionalism will have to offer some account of what a convention is and of how conventions may arise. Accordingly, after Syverson lays out Quine's attack upon Conventionalism in Chapter 1, in the next few chapters he sets about providing a characterization of conventional behavior, basically arguing that we should understand conventions in terms of coordination problems.

In Chapter 2, Syverson introduces some basic game-theoretic concepts and considers a number of different coordination problems. The upshot of his discussion is that the expectations of game-players themselves play a large role in determining what counts as a coordination problem and what counts as its solution.

In Chapter 3, Syverson addresses David Lewis' treatment of convention in terms of coordination equilibria. While Lewis himself abandoned this approach, arguing that it gives sufficient but not necessary conditions for something being a convention, Syverson argues that Lewis is mistaken here. More precisely, Syverson describes how the sort of cases which Lewis thinks count against a coordination equilibria account of convention can, after all, be understood as coordination problems.

In Chapter 4, Syverson returns to the role that player-expectations, and common knowledge of these, play in coordination problems. We obviously need some account of what the requisite common knowledge amounts to and how it might be achieved. Syverson begins by introducing and criticizing some of the standard accounts of common knowledge in terms of hierarchies, fixed-points, shared-situations, etc. In order to illustrate his own favored approach, Syverson then proceeds to consider the coordinated attack problem. This problem is usually considered unsolvable. Not so, Syverson argues. In fact, it is quite possible for the attacking generals to achieve a situation of mutual belief, which resolves their coordination problem.

Chapter 5 explores the notion of mutual belief. Syverson considers how mutual belief may come to constitute common knowledge. And he explains how, for the attacking generals facing the coordinated attack problem, a mutual belief that both generals will attack yields common knowledge between them to the effect that they will attack.

The natural question that arises at this point is how a situation of mutual understanding could ever be achieved in the first place. Syverson tackles this question in Chapter 6. Determinate common knowledge can determinately be achieved as long as the *criteria* that determine at what point common knowledge has been achieved are themselves kept vague. Syverson goes on to show how shared epistemic situations can arise, which suffice to yield a situation of common knowledge.

In the next three chapters Syverson is concerned with formally representing his shared situation account of common knowledge. Chapter 7 develops a *Logic of Familiarity*, aimed at capturing the sense of *know*, in which we know those things with which we are familiar. Little, if any, work has been done in this field and Syverson's account provides an interesting and invaluable contribution to this area of epistemic logic. Chapter 8 contains an extended discussion of epistemic logics. And in Chapter 9, Syverson presents a *Logic of Awareness*, which can be used to finitely capture common knowledge and which captures a number of the central features of epistemic awareness. As with his Logic of Familiarity, Syverson's Logic of Awareness provides an interesting and invaluable contribution to a little-developed field within epistemic logic.

In the final two chapters Syverson returns to the philosophical issues which motivated his project. Syverson argues that his brand of Conventionalism does not presuppose that those establishing the conventions need be credited with any prior grasp of logic. He counter's Quine by arguing that Conventionalism can offer a plausible evolutionary story about how and why logical behavior might have come about, considering, for example, the signaling behavior of Vervet monkeys from a developmental perspective.

Syverson concludes by considering the vexed question of how we are to understand rival systems of logic and their competing claims to truth. Here, interestingly enough, Conventionalism promises illumination, for if we view rival logicians as partaking in different conventions we are able to explain why deviant logics might arise. And we are not immediately forced to brand the rival logics we reject irrational. Syverson concludes with a discussion of whether or not a system of logic can be mistaken.

I hope that the preceding discussion has made it clear that *Logic, Convention, and Common Knowledge* is a very significant work that makes some real and ingenious contributions to a wide variety of issues. Despite its originality and sophistication, Syverson's discussion of logic, convention, and common knowledge is sufficiently accessible for this book to be used as a graduate-level introductory text. The book will be of great interest to logicians, philosophers, and computer scientists. It should most certainly be read by anyone who has an interest in the philosophy of logic.

Anthony Everett, Illinois State University

Acknowledgments

Thanks to Mike Dunn, who first suggested to me that there might be a book in these musings. Thanks to Raymond Smullyan, for helpful discussions and as one of the inspirations who first drew me to logic. In his honor I also state both that I believe each and every thing I have written herein and that I believe that some of the things I have written herein are false. Thanks to Nino Cocchiarella for helpful comments on an early draft, and to Anthony Everett for extensive and helpful comments on a more recent one. For now ancient but helpful discussions I thank Martín Abadi, Tim Day, Jim Gray (no not that one, James W. Gray, III), John McLean, Ed Mares, Einar Snekkenes, and Mark Tuttle. I thank assorted colleagues and coauthors for patience when other important things were set aside while I worked on this book, most notably Cathy Meadows. I thank Chris Sosa, for much helpful advice and patient guidance through the editorial process. I have waited so long to write this acknowledgment that I am sure I have forgotten some who helped me greatly in some way. I apologize for the oversight and thank you for your contribution.

Last and foremost I thank my family: for inspiration, for peopling the examples herein, and especially for patience with the time this took and, even more so, the energy and attention. Thank You.

1

Conventionalism: Setting Out the Problem

Logic is conventional. On some interpretations this claim is almost universally accepted. Such interpretations are also widely dismissed as trivial. Other interpretations, generally seen as making this a more substantive claim, are generally seen as making this a false claim. The view set out below will probably please neither the proponents nor the detractors of conventionalism. The notion of convention I will defend bears a resemblance to the 'trivial' interpretations, but I will contend ultimately that it is not trivial. My goal in this chapter is simply to set out the classic view of conventionalism and the standard arguments against it. In subsequent chapters I will explore alternatives and their implications.

Conventionalism in one form or another can be traced back at least to Hobbes. (For example, cf. Kneale and Kneale 1962, 1984.) Some find elements of conventionalism in Occam and even Aristotle (Giannoni 1971, pp. 14–ff.). I do not intend to trace the historical roots of conventionalism and thus begin at a much later date. Still, one must choose somewhere to begin, and I choose to begin with Carnap. If this choice is somewhat arbitrary, at least it is conventionally so. For, discussion of conventionalism in this century has largely derived from his conception. Indeed, the principal arguments against conventionalism were given by Quine in response to *The Logical Syntax of Language* (Carnap 1937). Since I intend to examine Quine's arguments, this is a good starting place, though Carnap also mentions convention earlier, in *The Logical Structure of the World* (Carnap 1928).

1.1 Carnap's Conventionalism

In *The Logical Syntax of Language*, Carnap sets out his Principle of Tolerance: "*It is not our business to set up prohibitions, but to arrive at conventions*" (Carnap 1937, §17). What he means by this is that we should not be interested in ruling out linguistic forms but in deciding which ones to use under which circumstances. Thus he continues, "*In logic, there are no morals.* Everyone is at liberty to build up his own logic, i.e. his own form of language, as he wishes. All that is required of him is that, if he wishes to discuss it, he must state his methods clearly, and give syntactic rules instead of philosophical arguments."

In his "Intellectual Autobiography", he explains that he was motivated here by the desire to demonstrate that philosophical controversies were often over linguistic usage. He offered in the Principle of Tolerance a means to solving many such controversies.

> For example, in the controversy about the foundations of mathematics, the conception of intuitionism may be construed as a proposal to restrict the means of expression and the means of deduction of the language of mathematics in a certain way, while the classical conception leaves the language unrestricted. I intended to make available in syntax the conceptual means for an exact formulation of controversies of this kind. Furthermore, I wished to show that everyone is free to choose the rules of his language and thereby his logic in any way he wishes. This I called the "principle of tolerance"; it might perhaps be called more exactly "the principle of conventionality of language forms". As a consequence, the discussion of controversies of the kind mentioned need only concern first, the syntactical properties of the various forms of language, and second, practical reasons for preferring one or the other form for given purposes. In this way, assertions that a particular language is the correct language or represents the correct logic such as often occurred in earlier discussions, are eliminated.... (Carnap 1963)

Not long after *The Logical Syntax of Language* was written Carnap realized that he had construed things too narrowly and that many of the problems that he had claimed were merely syntactic also had semantic or pragmatic elements. This comes out in a way relevant to our current concerns in §12 of *Foundations of Logic and Mathematics* (Carnap 1939). He addresses there the question of whether or not logic is a matter of convention and answers that it depends what is meant by the claim.

Certainly one is free to choose any syntax one wants for an uninterpreted system, and there can be no right or wrong to the matter. What system one chooses will limit the semantic interpretations one can give for that system, but the prior choice of syntax is still arbitrary.

Thus, a sentential language cannot express everything expressible in a first order language. But, the rules of deduction we choose for any such language will always be interpretable (subject to any consistency constraints we impose, etc.)

On the other hand if we impose an interpretation on our language prior to deciding on our logical rules, then we are constrained in a way we were not previously. We can see the two options here as an ordering of decisions. That is, we can proceed by giving formation rules of the language, then transformation rules, and then give an interpretation. Alternatively, we can give the formation rules, then an interpretation (or perhaps set of acceptable interpretations), and then the transformation rules. If we proceed the first way, then the logical, i.e. transformational, rules may be arbitrarily given. If we proceed the second way, then they may not, at least not if we want them to have the usual properties such as being truth preserving.[1]

It appears that whether or not we take logic to be conventional turns on the order of our metatheoretical decisions, to use Carnap's terminology. However, Carnap points out that even should we decide to precede transformation rules with semantic interpretation, there is still a fundamental element of convention; "for the basis on which logic is constructed, namely, the interpretation of the logical signs (e.g., by a determination of truth conditions) can be freely chosen." We might add that on a *meta*metatheoretical level we are also free to choose the order in which to proceed. Thus, from a Carnapian point of view, we could say that whether or not logic is conventional is itself a matter of convention.

This entire discussion may strike some as having started off on the wrong foot. What is all this talk of decisions in constructing or interpreting a language? Aren't we interested in *the* logical properties? It hardly seems fair in assessing the conventionalism of logic to accept at the outset arbitrary formal systems; to do so would be question begging. If we are to accept a formal system, it should be because it captures the logical properties; we don't want to say that the logical properties are the logical properties because they're the ones reflected by the formal system we chose, do we? Well, yes and no. But, we are getting slightly ahead of ourselves. For now we simply note that to talk of *the* logical properties without the possibility of alternative is to simply preclude a conventional account of logic, at least in the ordinary sense. Thus, putting things this way simply begs the same question the

---

[1] Recall that not all rules are meant to be truth preserving. E.g., in modal logic necessitation is validity preserving but not truth preserving (Fagin et al. 1990).

conventionalist was accused of begging—with the opposite answer.

Before leaving Carnap we make two observations that should probably be kept in mind when considering his work in connection with the issues of the last paragraph. First, Carnap's focus on artificial languages was a feature of his overall logical empiricism. His conventionalism arose from this rather than vice versa. Second, Carnap accepted the challenge to address both natural and artificial languages and attempted to do this (Carnap 1955). Admittedly, this paper deals primarily with analyticity on the level of terms and predication. Thus, it would not be a complete account of the logical properties of natural languages even if it were entirely correct; however, it was not meant to be a complete account, though Carnap thought such an account was possible. While significant, exploring these points would take us too far afield from our present interests. We now turn to Quine's treatment of convention.

1.2 Quine: The Standard View

If anything qualifies as the standard view of conventionalism, it is probably a version that centers on the notion of logical truth as some sort of truth by convention. This is exactly the view addressed by Quine's famous essay of that name (Quine 1936). The arguments he gives there are the ones usually given, either implicitly or explicitly, by anyone who rejects a conventional account of logic. Thus, it is important that we consider them.

A difficulty of "Truth by Convention" is that nowhere therein does Quine tell us what a convention is. In his autobiography, he indicates that the paper was drawn from lectures he had given on *The Logical Syntax of Language*, which gives us some indication of his motivation (Quine 1985, pp. 121–2). He also presents examples of a number of different types of conventions. Citing Russell, he begins by telling us that, "[a] definition, strictly is a convention of notational abbreviation" (*op. cit.*, p. 78). But, even if definition is a convention, not all conventions are definitions. "[If] we are to construe logic also as true by convention, we must rest logic ultimately upon some manner of convention other than definition: for it was noted earlier that definitions are available only for transforming truths, not for founding them." (p. 88) He then proceeds to give us some of these other conventions. They generally have the form

> Let all results of putting a statement for 'p', a statement for 'q', ... in _____ be true.

where in the place of _____ is an axiom of logic expressed in terms of 'p', 'q', ... There are others of slightly different form, e.g. one to capture *modus ponens*. But, we needn't go into detail here. What we are interested in is the general concept of convention that Quine has in mind, and the above is sufficient for this purpose.

The concept of convention that emerges from Quine's exposition is that of either definitional abbreviations or stipulative rules. What is common to both of these, and to the standard view generally, is a requirement of explicitness. Whatever logical conventions we use must be given overtly. The vicious justificatory regress that results from such explicit conventionalism was well illustrated as far back as last century in Lewis Carroll's "What the Tortoise Said to Achilles".[2] This remains one of the clearest illustrations of the regress, and Quine himself acknowledges that the relevant part of his critique has this form. We give a brief statement of Carroll's classic story.

The Tortoise has Achilles write down the following:

(A) Things that are equal to the same are equal to each other.
(B) The two sides of this triangle are things equal to the same.
(Z) The two sides of this triangle are equal to each other.

Achilles then allows that the Tortoise might accept A and B as true and yet reject the "Hypothetical Proposition" that,

(C) If A and B are true, Z must be true.

He also allows that the Tortoise is not "*as yet* under any logical necessity to accept Z as true." In order to force the Tortoise to accept Z, logically based on what has already been given, he appeals to

(D) If A and B and C are true, Z must be true.

Alas, poor Achilles. While the Tortoise agrees that if he were to accept the truth of D along with that of A, B, and C, then he would be logically required to accept the truth of Z, he adds that he is as yet under no logical obligation to accept D. Something more is needed, ... and they are off and running again.

We can agree with the Tortoise that one might call for justification of the inference from A and B to Z before accepting Z, but we can also question whether or not the only possible form of justification is another premise. It is possible to reject, in effect, the request for justification. Black (1970a) argues that "an apparent request for justification of *modus ponens* has to be met, not by an answer, but by a demonstration that the question is illegitimate" (p. 22). However, rather than

---

[2]This paper originally appeared in *Mind* 4, 1895 pp. 278–280. All references to it made herein are to its appearance in Carroll 1977, which also contains a discussion of it. Another analysis of Quine's argument with respect to the Achilles-Tortoise dialogue is that of Giannoni (1971, pp. 58–ff.).

saving conventionalism, this preempts it:

> As to a possible charge of conventionalism, I may point out that it is no part of the view that I am presenting that *modus ponens* is "true by convention" or something of that sort. For if there can be no question of *choosing* to adopt the rule, as I have been contending, there can be no question either of adopting a convention or coming to an agreement that the rule shall hold. If conventionalism means to imply such a choice, or agreement, or convention, its very formulation involves a logical absurdity. Far from advocating a form of conventionalism, then, I am denying that any form of conventionalism can make sense. (*ibid.*)

Of course Black is just observing the absurdity in the Tortoise's requests for justification. But, before accepting the charge of absurdity, we should be sure that this is the only form that conventionalism can take. We will return to this (and to Quine) presently; however, before leaving this example we set aside a specific peculiarity of it that doesn't concern us.

Since our concern here is only with the conventionalism of logic, it is also only with the truths *of logic*. The inference from A and B to Z is certainly mathematically justified; however, depending on how one treats equality and on one's views of the relationship between mathematics and logic, one might not think that it is logically justified. For the moment let us set aside these issues and focus on an inference which is uncontroversially logical, viz that from A, B, and C to Z. This is clearly just an instance of modus ponens. So, let us start the actual regress one step further along.

This is a restriction that we also apply to our comments about Quine and other authors. In writings on conventionalism one often finds reference to the truths of "logic and mathematics". We will not pursue the issue of the relation between logic and mathematics in this work. Thus, unless otherwise noted, claims are meant to apply to logic. Whether or not any of them apply to mathematics as well is an issue we leave for others.

As we just noted, we must be sure that conventionalism must have this explicit form before accepting that it involves a vicious regress. There may yet be ways around this. Quine (1936) points out that if truth assignments were made one at a time there would be no problem with conventional agreement about the truths of logic (p. 105). They could "simply be asserted by fiat." But, conventions of the form necessary for finitely capturing all of the logical truths amount to instructions for making infinitely many truth assignments. Thus, logical truths must be *inferred* from these general instructions. Since these inferences are presumably logical, they must themselves be conventional or instances of a convention. And, since there are infinitely many truth assignments prescribed by the original convention, there are infinitely many of these conventional inferences. Thus, in order for these inferences to be captured finitely, there must be at least one other convention which gives instructions for making infinitely many truth assignments. But then each instance of a logical truth based on this convention must be inferred, thus giving rise to still another convention.... Thus it seems that explicit conventionalism does indeed involve us in a vicious regress; however, we have not yet explored the possibility of alternatives to explicitness.

1.3 As-ifism

> Quine is not merely making the obvious point that the axioms and inference procedures which constitute logic and mathematics did not (as a matter of contingent historical fact) arise through a process of explicit legislation. No one supposes that some ancient pre-Babylonian monarch bestowed logic upon a world which had previously been devoid of it by means of a Codex. What the empiricists recommended was that we give up thinking about natural language in philosophy, and consider a rational reconstruction. Conventionalism was a form of 'as-ifism'. Carnap said in effect, that our language is *as if* logic and mathematics had come into existence through the adoption of a set of conventions. Quine's point is that this story is incoherent even as makebelieve. Logic and mathematics *could not have* come into existence as the result of the adoption of conventions. (Putnam 1983, pp. 172–173)

There is one point of scholarship to make before responding to the substance of what says here: nowhere in the writings of Carnap could I find a statement, either explicit or implicit, advocating the "as-ifism" Putnam attributes to him. I do not claim to know what Carnap would put in place of this. In fact, given that there is nothing invalid in the Quinean critique of explicit conventionalism, the only viable solution I see is to bite the bullet of as-ifism. But, I am not Rudolf Carnap and do not know what clever ideas he might have applied to issues he never addressed. Thus, given that Putnam finds as-ifism untenable, it is uncharitable for him to attribute such a position to Carnap without textual support.

Putnam has not only overstated Carnap here; he has misconstrued Quine as well. It is true that Quine rejects not only that logic is explicitly given by conventions, but also that it could arise from conventions discovered *ex post facto* by "rational reconstruction". But, he rejects each of them for different reasons. As we have seen, in the case of explicitly given conventions, Quine correctly demonstrates that we become involved in a vicious regress. In the case of rationally reconstructed conventions, Quine claims not viciousness, but vacuity.

> [W]hen a convention is incapable of being communicated until after its adoption, its role is not so clear. In dropping the attributes of deliberateness and explicitness from the notion of linguistic convention we risk depriving the latter of any explanatory force and reducing it to an idle label. We may wonder what one adds to the bare statement that the truths of logic and mathematics are a priori, or to the still barer behavioristic statement that they are firmly accepted, when he characterizes them as true by convention in such a sense. (Quine 1936, p. 106)

Far from rejecting as-ifism for linguistic conventions, Quine states that "this account accords well with what we actually do. We discourse without phrasing the conventions; afterwards, in writings such as this, we formulate them to fit our behavior." (*ibid.*, p. 105) Quine's complaint rests not with as-ifism per se, but with as-ifism that is essentially so. Conventions that might have been explicitly given beforehand, but were not, are perfectly acceptable to Quine. He objects to convention that is "incapable of being communicated until after its adoption." Further, his objection is not that convention in this sense is incoherent; rather it is that we gain nothing from the postulation of such convention. Below, we will develop the machinery to defend just such conventions against just such objections: I intend to show that essential as-ifism is not only tenable but useful too.

1.4 Prospectus

This inquiry will look at convention, coordinated action, and common knowledge. We are motivated partly by an attempt to deal with the issues raised above, but we are also motivated simply by an attempt to further explicate these concepts. Our next goal is to take a closer look at what a convention is, in other words what is involved when a behavior is deemed conventional. This will require the use of some game-theoretic concepts. Thus, we will set these out before proceeding to convention itself. The basic account of convention will also assume that those playing the game have certain mutual expectations. It is accounting for these that will lead us into epistemic issues. Specifically it will require an account of common knowledge. Our discussion of common knowledge will tie back to earlier chapters in several ways. First, it will be a necessary ingredient for the forming of mutual expectations. Second, it will be closely tied to coordination, which will also have been a primary ingredient in our account of convention. Third, it will be seen to involve the finite capture of an apparently infinite number of inferences. In exploring these areas, we will examine in some detail a problem from the distributed computing literature, the coordinated attack problem. It has long been thought that this problem is unsolvable; it has even been proven to be unsolvable. Nonetheless, we will show that, appropriately understood, it is solvable after all.

We next turn to logic. A main motivation for so doing is to formally capture the epistemic concepts introduced in chapter 4 and further explored in chapters 5 and 6. The logic of familiarity, set out in chapter 7, is a logic that makes sentences true or false only when the terms in them refer to familiar individuals; otherwise they are undefined. By 'familiar' we mean simply that the terms are somehow meaningful to the knower. This logic thus captures at least one of the aspects of what is actually known by anyone; they are only familiar with a finite number of individuals. We also present an associated possible world semantics with respect to which the logic is shown to be sound and complete.

Chapter 8 sets out the issues in going from epistemic logic based on a semantics using traditional, alethic possible worlds to a more cognitive semantics using more epistemic worlds. The logic of familiarity given in chapter 7 is a first step from the traditional in that it does distinguish between familiar and unfamiliar terms. However, about formulae containing only familiar terms reasoners are logically omniscient.

One reason we move to epistemic from traditional worlds is that it lets us represent in a formal logic a natural characterization of common knowledge (shared situations). This characterization captures common knowledge in a finite way that other characterizations seem to miss. More generally, it fits the view we are espousing: our intent in this book is to characterize logic as arising from the finite collective interaction of finite entities. Furthermore, in any cognitively realistic sense, people know only finitely many things. Thus, if we are to realistically capture reasoning about common knowledge by such reasoners, it ought to be finitely expressible, and the semantic characterization of the knowledge of reasoners should also be finite.

Chapter 9 sets out a logic of awareness, roughly one reasoning about the concept of a proposition being familiar. It is this logic that is capable of providing a logical explication of common knowledge as just mentioned. We prove that it is sound and complete with respect to the situation semantics we use to characterize common knowledge in chapter 4. Since this is the logic that 'does the job' the reader might bypass chapters 7 and 8 without completely losing the central thread of our presentation. Indeed, those embracing from the start a situational view of logic may think these chapters a slight diversion. However, these chapters follow a natural path from traditional possible worlds to something more in keeping with the cognitive capabilities of real world possessors of knowledge. Certainly it is not the first path blazed from worlds to situations or similar structures, but it is one that actually arose in the course of this study. Thus, you can bypass those chapters and still reach the goal but only if you don't mind missing part of the journey.

In the last two chapters we return to the questions with which we began. We use the characterizations of convention and common knowledge developed in the earlier chapters to answer the criticisms and questions that Quine has raised about a conventional account of logic.

2
Games and Equilibria

As I remarked in the previous chapter, Quine nowhere tells us explicitly what a convention is; though we get a pretty clear picture from his examples and analysis. If we are to resolve the issues raised above, we will have to be more precise in specifying convention than the above authors. A sustained attempt to do just that was given by Lewis (1969). Lewis's basic idea is to treat conventions as game-theoretic coordination equilibria. What this means will be explained below. To give the flavor of the idea we begin with a standard example from Schelling (1960).

Suppose two people have the goal of meeting somewhere in New York City. The only goal is that they both go to the same place; it does not matter what place that is. Where should they go?[3] It seems that in order to solve this problem, the people must have common knowledge of where they should meet. They could just end up at, e.g., Saint Patrick's Cathedral because one is a Catholic prone to going to the main church in a given archdiocese while the other is unfamiliar with any other New York landmark. They have not so much solved the coordination problem as lucked onto the answer. (Compare the 'solutions' two people give to a complicated mathematical problem: one painstakingly works out the calculations while the other simply correctly guesses that the answer is $7\pi/9$ because that is the first value on the page of a book he has open in front of him.) But, should they somehow on repeated occasions meet at Saint Patrick's, each expecting the other to be there, and each expecting the other to expect him to be there, etc., then they would be meeting there by convention.

In order to give a precise characterization of what is demonstrated

---

[3]Schelling actually presented this problem to an unscientifically selected sample of people in New Haven, CT. An absolute majority of those sampled settled on the information booth at Grand Central Station, which is the station from which trains depart New York for Connecticut (*op. cit.*, p. 55). 'Easier' problems had even higher degrees of agreement.

by this example we will need to spell out a number of technical notions. That is the primary purpose of this chapter.

The first notion we need to set out formally is that of a game. We describe here the classical idea of a mathematical game as set out by von Neumann and Morgenstern (1944), Luce and Raiffa (1957), Thomas (1984), and Osborne and Rubinstein (1994). Results presented here will be given without proof or detailed explanation. See the above works for details and/or references on where to find such details. To simplify matters we begin by describing a **two-person game**. We can generalize to n-person games, but many results become much more complex. Games have two players, whom we shall call 'Row 'and 'Column' because of the way their options will be represented. Each of them has a finite number of **pure strategies** to follow. A pure strategy can be thought of as a deterministic list of moves a player would make in response to a particular list of moves by his opponent. In the simplest case it might consist of a single move, for example putting out one finger in a game of Odd-or-Even. Alternatively, it may consist of the list of moves one side would make in an entire chess game. These options are assumed to be known to each player. Until a strategy is chosen neither Row nor Column knows which option the other will choose. Each pairwise combination of optional strategies determines an **outcome**. Thus, in a simple case where Row's options are $R1$ and $R2$ and Column's options are $C1$ and $C2$ there are four possible outcomes: $(R1, C1)$, $(R1, C2)$, $(R2, C1)$, and $(R2, C2)$. Each player attaches a **utility** to each of the outcomes. This can all be concisely represented in a **payoff matrix**. For example,

	$C1$	$C2$
$R1$	3 −1	1 −3
$R2$	1 −1	−2 3

In the game represented here, to the outcome $(R2, C1)$ Row attaches a utility of −1, whereas Column attaches a utility of 1. Utilities are not to be thought of as absolute: they are only meant to indicate relative preferences for outcomes. (They are also relative to the individual, i.e., we cannot compare utility values between individuals.) Thus, in the above game, given that he adopted strategy $R2$, Row would have preferred that Column had adopted strategy $C2$. We can see this because the value Row attaches to $(R2, C2)$ is higher than the value he attaches to $(R2, C1)$. Column, on the other hand, prefers to play $C1$ over $C2$ in this case.

2.1 Games of Conflict – Games of Coordination

The stereotypical game is the game of pure conflict. What makes it a game of pure conflict is that each outcome is such that one player wins exactly to the extent that the other one loses. A good example of a game of pure conflict is poker. If our measure of utility is the money changing hands, then one player gains exactly to the extent that others lose—though he need not win everything from a single other player.[4] These are thus also known as zero-sum games because in each case the values of an outcome for the players sum to zero (possibly only after normalization of their utility functions). These games are the most theoretically well understood. Most of the results concerning zero-sum games were set out in the first major work on the subject (von Neumann and Morgenstern 1944).

The alternative to a zero-sum game is cleverly called a 'nonzero-sum game', or, as Schelling (1960) more descriptively puts it, "a mutual-dependence game". In mutual-dependence games conflict may still predominate, but there is also at least some need for cooperation or mutual accommodation. Consider the following standard scene from assorted adventure movies: the hero and a villain are fighting each other while the car they are driving careens along a mountain road. From time to time they interrupt their fight and work together to keep the car from flying off a cliff or into the side of the mountain. If either of them were to focus solely on defeating the other, they would both perish. Though perhaps difficult to formalize, this captures very well the notion of a mutual-dependence game.

While nonzero-sum games are all and only those involving some degree of mutual dependence, these games may also involve some degree of conflict, as the above example illustrates. In the extreme case of

---
[4]We should be careful to observe that incomparability of interpersonal utilities applies here as anywhere. It may seem that each player attaches the same value to a dollar, and, as I said, one gains exactly to the extent another loses. However, if we are being precise, we should say that they have the exact same preference ordering on outcomes. Thus, these orderings can be normalized (i.e., placed on a uniform scale) most conveniently to one dollar equals one unit of utility.

no conflict we have a game where the preferences of the players coincide exactly. Dividing mutual-dependence games in this way leaves us with a tripartite distinction of game types: (1) zero-sum or pure conflict games, (2) mixed-motive games, and (3) games with pure coincidence of interest. It is with games of this third type (and games of the second type close to the third, i.e., in which coincidence of interest predominates) that we will be fundamentally concerned while setting out Lewis's characterization of convention .

2.2 Equilibria and Solutions of Games

The next notions we need to set out are those of a game solution and a game equilibrium. As with many other features of game theory, the notions are simple in the two-person zero-sum case but become quite complex once we stray from that case. We introduce the notion of a solution via the "Minimax Theorem" of von Neumann. First, we need the concept of a **mixed strategy**. If a player has n pure strategies in the sense set out above, then a mixed strategy is represented as an n-tuple, $(p_1, \ldots, p_n)$, where p_i is the probability that that player plays pure strategy i.[5] Let $e_R(x, y)$ be the utility that Row attaches to his playing x and Column's playing y. Similarly, let $e_C(x, y)$ be the utility that Column attaches to that result. We can then state the following basic theorem of von Neumann (1937).

Theorem 1 *Consider a finite two-person zero-sum game (i.e., one where each player has a fixed finite number of pure strategies). Let X and Y be the sets of all possible mixed strategies for Row and Column respectively. Then,*

$$\max_{x \in X} \min_{y \in Y} e_R(x, y) = \min_{y \in Y} \max_{x \in X} e_R(x, y)$$
$$= -(\max_{y \in Y} \min_{x \in X} e_C(x, y)) = -(\min_{x \in X} \max_{y \in Y} e_C(x, y))$$

What this theorem says is that if Row maximizes his minimum payoff and Column minimizes Row's maximum payoff, the resulting expected value (utility) is the same. And, this value is the negative of the payoff if Column maximizes his minimum utility or Row minimizes Column's maximum utility. Furthermore, the strategy Row follows in maximizing his own minimum payoff will also minimize Column's maximum payoff, and the same goes *mutatis mutandis* for Column's strategies. Let x^* and y^* be such strategies for Row and Column respectively. These are

---

[5]There are questions about the reasonability of mixed strategies (e.g., Do they make any sense for games that are played only once?) that we will not explore here.

called **optimal strategies**. The utility that results from playing them (ignoring sign) is called **the value of the game**. And, a pair of optimal strategies together with the value of a game is called a **solution** to that game. If the utilities that a player attaches to each outcome induces a linear ordering on his strategies for each strategy of his opponent, then the solution is unique in that there is a unique pair of optimal strategies.

Note that if one of the players is playing an optimal strategy, it will not pay the other to switch from his optimal strategy. By switching he can only do as well or worse. We can give a precise characterization of such a pair of strategies into which the players settle. Let X and Y be sets of available strategies for Row and Column respectively. An **equilibrium** is a pair of strategies $x^* \in X$ and $y^* \in Y$ such that for all $x \in X$ and $y \in Y$,

$$e_R(x, y^*) \leq e_R(x^*, y^*)$$
and
$$e_C(x^*, y) \leq e_C(x^*, y^*)$$

It may seem as though we are introducing unnecessary terminological redundancy here. Aren't pairs of optimal strategies and equilibrium pairs just the same thing? Apparently they are: observe the following theorem.

Theorem 2 *A pair of strategies in a finite two-person zero-sum game is an equilibrium iff each of the strategies is optimal.*

This theorem equates optimal strategies and equilibria, but only in the zero-sum case. In the nonzero-sum case things do not always work out so neatly. And, recall that it is with nonzero-sum cases that we are ultimately primarily concerned. To see that optimal strategies and equilibria need not coincide, consider the following game in which there is a pure coincidence of interests.

	$C1$	$C2$
$R1$	2 2	3 3
$R2$	1 1	4 4

Row's optimal strategy, the one that maximizes his minimum payoff is $R1$. Column's optimal strategy is $C2$. Thus, $(R1, C2)$ is the only pair of optimal strategies. But, the only equilibrium pair is $(R2, C2)$. So, we can see that in a nonzero-sum game optimal strategies do not necessarily yield equilibria, even though there is complete agreement between the players on the preference ordering of outcomes. One of the things this example demonstrates is that pure coincidence of interests does not guarantee cooperation. Despite this coincidence of interests, this game has no solution in the sense defined above. There are other types of solution we might explore, but we will not do so. In our effort to understand convention, equilibria of games are more significant than solutions. We will discuss why this is so below.

The above example has an equilibrium even if it lacks a solution. Are there perhaps finite two-person nonzero-sum games that have no equilibria as well? No. The following theorem was proven by Nash (1953).

Theorem 3 *Any two-person game with a finite number of pure strategies has at least one equilibrium.*

What about the n-person case? Unfortunately there is no fully general theorem corresponding to the one above. Nash (1951) proved a somewhat general theorem. But, before we can discuss it we must set out the notion of an equilibrium for an n-person game. An **equilibrium** in an n-person game is an n-tuple of strategies $(x_1^*, \ldots, x_n^*)$ such that player i plays strategy x_i^* and such that for all other strategies $y_1, \ldots, y_n$:

$$e_i(x_1^*, \ldots, x_i^*, \ldots, x_n^*) \geq e_i(x_1^*, \ldots, y_i, \ldots, x_n^*) \qquad \text{for } 1 \leq i \leq n$$

Nash (1951) discussed the theory of n-person games when there is no cooperation between players. Once we allow cooperation players may form coalitions and may thus play strategies not in their immediate best interest because they may receive side payments from the coalition. Once cooperation is allowed things quickly get complicated. However, for non-cooperative games, Nash was able to show the following.

Theorem 4 *In any non-cooperative n-person game where each player has a finite number of pure strategies, there is always an equilibrium.*

This theorem may seem insignificant for our purposes. For, in establishing a convention we would expect people to try to cooperate as much as possible. However, many conventions may arise without explicit communication of intended strategies to other players. Indeed, logical conventions would have to be largely established this way initially. Also the possibility of coalitions may not be all that significant.

For instance, if there is a pure coincidence of interests it should be clear that no player can improve his payoffs by forming a coalition. Thus, such a game is reducible to a non-cooperative game. So,

Theorem 5 *Any finite n-person game in which the preferences of players exactly coincide has an equilibrium.*

Though trivial to prove, this theorem is significant. For, it shows us that arbitrary finite groups can attain equilibria when their interests coincide. We cannot expect there to be pure coincidence of interests when a convention is established. But, we would certainly expect a preponderance of interest. This theorem shows us that at least in the limiting case there is always an equilibrium.

Lewis (1969) tells us that he is only interested in "situations in which coincidence of interest predominates: that is, in which the differences between different agents' payoffs in any one square (perhaps after suitable linear rescaling) are small compared to some of the differences between payoffs in different squares" (p. 14). Since Lewis ultimately makes this a necessary condition for conventions, it would be nice to have a precise statement of it. I propose the following.

Let us say that the interests of all the players in a game **approximately coincide** if for any players $i, j \in S$ and outcome $\bar{x}$ there exists outcomes $\bar{y}$ and $\bar{z}$ such that $|e_i(\bar{x}) - e_j(\bar{x})| < |e_i(\bar{y}) - e_j(\bar{z})|$. It is unclear whether or not there is a version of Nash's theorem for finite n-person games in which the interests of players approximately coincide. We may have to say something about the nature of the coalitions that can form (e.g., are side payments allowed?) and about the nature of the coordination that players can adopt (e.g., can they jointly randomize their strategies?) in order to get a provable theorem. Fortunately, we need not worry about this since we are not specifically concerned with the necessary and sufficient conditions for a game to have an equilibrium. We will be restricting our attention to (some of) those that do have equilibria, regardless of whether we can decide this for an arbitrary game of a given type.

We have yet to explicitly tie conventions to equilibria. We still have a few more notions to set out before we can state Lewis's characterization of convention, but we can now give one of the main ingredients.

2.3 Coordination Problems

One of the key parts of convention is coordination between participants. The actual convention arrived at does not matter to those participants. What matters is that they 'get together' in some way while engaging in an activity. Thus, the two people in the beginning of this chapter

18 / LOGIC, CONVENTION, AND COMMON KNOWLEDGE

do not care where they meet provided *that* they meet. The reason we have been discussing game-theoretic equilibria is that certain of them will serve as solutions to just such coordination problems.

Perhaps being a game-theoretic equilibrium is sufficient for being a solution to a coordination problem. Lewis gives us an example (*op. cit.*, pp. 15–16) to show that this is not so. Suppose that there are four places that two people might meet. They would like to meet at any of the first three places. They also like going to the fourth place, each by himself. The fourth place is not good as a meeting place and each finds that the presence of the other detracts from his pleasure at being there. Clearly, if both arrive at the fourth place, it would not be reasonable to call this 'a coordination' on their part. To reflect this state of affairs Lewis gives the following payoff matrix.

	$C1$	$C2$	$C3$	$C4$
$R1$	1 meet 1	0 0	0 0	.5 0
$R2$	0 0	1 meet 1	0 0	.5 0
$R3$	0 0	0 0	1 meet 1	.5 0
$R4$	0 .5	0 .5	0 .5	.2 meet .2

According to the definition $(R4, C4)$ is an equilibrium point even though it does not seem reasonable to call it a 'coordination'. To avoid such problems, Lewis defines a **coordination equilibrium** to be an outcome "in which no one would have been better off had *any one* agent alone acted otherwise, either himself or someone else" (p. 14). According to this definition $(R1, C1)$, $(R2, C2)$, and $(R3, C3)$ are coordination equilibria, but $(R4, C4)$ is not.

While this definition seems reasonable, and we will in fact continue to use it, we must be cautious about assuming that it completely captures our intuitions about the difference between ordinary equilibria and coordination equilibria. Consider the following two scenarios.

Scenario 1. Row and Column would be happy to meet in any one of three places. There is also a fourth place that each would be just as happy to go to as he would be were he to meet in any of the first three places. This fourth place is useless as a meeting place, but it is just as desirable a place to go whether or not the other person is there.

Scenario 2. Row and Column would be happy to meet in any one of three places. There is also a fourth place that each would be just as happy to go to alone as he would be were he to meet in any of the first three places with the other. However, should the two arrive at this fourth place together, the value it has to each of them individually is completely obliterated. (Perhaps each is too distracted or embarrassed by the other to pursue his original purpose in the presence of the other.) Nonetheless, it is just as acceptable a meeting place as the other three.

Both of these may be reasonably accurately captured by the following payoff matrix. And, in this matrix $(R4, C4)$ is as much a coordination equilibrium according to the definition as are $(R1, C1)$, $(R2, C2)$, and $(R3, C3)$. But, while in Scenario 2 it seems reasonable to claim that the two have coordinated by going to $(R4, C4)$, in Scenario 1 such a claim does not seem reasonable.

	$C1$	$C2$	$C3$	$C4$
$R1$	1 / meet / 1	0 / 0	0 / 0	1 / 0
$R2$	0 / 0	1 / meet / 1	0 / 0	1 / 0
$R3$	0 / 0	0 / 0	1 / meet / 1	1 / 0
$R4$	0 / 1	0 / 1	0 / 1	1 / meet / 1

One can readily see from the matrix that each of the players would do well to play his fourth strategy, regardless of what the other one does. There need be no attempt to coordinate. A way of revising our formal criterion is available to get around this difficulty. Lewis defines a **proper coordination equilibrium** to be a coordination equilibrium that each player strictly prefers to any other outcome that he could attain given the other players' choices. This rules out $(R4, C4)$ as a *proper* coordination equilibrium. (In fact it rules out all the equilibria in this game.) Have we now completely captured intuitive coordination? Consider the following.

Scenario 3. Row and Column would be happy to meet in any one of three places. There is also a fourth place that each would like to go to alone, though not as much as he would like to meet in any of the first three places with the other. However, should the two arrive at this fourth place together, the value it has to each of them individually is completely obliterated. (Perhaps each is too distracted by the other or too embarrassed to pursue his original purpose in the presence of the other.) Nonetheless, the fourth place *qua* meeting place is actually preferable to the other three for both of them. We might represent this situation by the following matrix.

	$C1$	$C2$	$C3$	$C4$
$R1$	.8 / meet / .8	0 / 0	0 / 0	.5 / 0
$R2$	0 / 0	.8 / meet / .8	0 / 0	.5 / 0
$R3$	0 / 0	0 / 0	.8 / meet / .8	.5 / 0
$R4$	0 / .5	0 / .5	0 / .5	1 / meet / 1

All of the outcomes along the diagonal are proper coordination equilibria. In fact, scenario 3, thus characterized, satisfies Lewis's definition of a **coordination problem**, viz: "situations of interdependent decision by two or more agents in which coincidence of interest predominates and in which there are two or more proper coordination equilibria" (p. 24).

The requirement that there be multiple proper coordination equilibria is to rule out cases that are trivial in the sense that, if there is a unique equilibrium, it will be reached "if the nature of the situation is clear enough so that everybody makes the best choice given his expectations, everybody expects everybody else to make the best choice given his expectations, and so on" (p. 16). Thus, there will be no need to coordinate, to make sure that the same equilibrium is reached.

The apparent problem with the definition is that, while scenario 3 satisfies it, it seems that both Row and Column should both go to the fourth place based simply on reasoning like that in the last paragraph. Thus, they would not be coordinating as it first appeared.

2.4 Solutions to Coordination Problems

We might notice that outcome $(R4, C4)$ is a maximin-maximin pair. It might seem that we should be focussed on these rather than equilibria after all, but that cannot be right. Recall the matrix

	$C1$	$C2$
$R1$	2 \ 2	3 \ 3
$R2$	1 \ 1	4 \ 4

Here the only maximin-maximin pair was $(R1, C2)$. But, it is clear that the unique equilibrium $(R2, C2)$ (which we can now see is a proper coordination equilibrium) not only serves to coordinate (uniqueness issues aside) but is the most desirable outcome for each of the players individually.

So, what other strategy should we seek in finding solutions to coordination problems? Perhaps the characterization is as yet inadequate.

We will reserve any serious criticism of Lewis's treatment. But, let us consider a potential fix to the problems with scenario 3.

In scenario 3, the fourth meeting place is actually preferred to the other three. Perhaps we should have a definition of 'coordination problem' in which there are two or more proper coordination equilibria all of which are equally valued by all players. Thus, in place of scenario 3 we have the following.

Scenario 4. This is exactly the same as scenario 3 except that all the meeting places are equally desirable to both Row and Column.

A reasonable payoff matrix for scenario 4 would thus be:

	$C1$	$C2$	$C3$	$C4$
$R1$	1 / meet / 1	0 / / 0	0 / / 0	.5 / / 0
$R2$	0 / / 0	1 / meet / 1	0 / / 0	.5 / / 0
$R3$	0 / / 0	0 / / 0	1 / meet / 1	.5 / / 0
$R4$	0 / / .5	0 / / .5	0 / / .5	1 / meet / 1

One difficulty with our current proposal is that it seems to undercut its own intention. Specifically, it would fail to distinguish scenario 4 from the following.

Scenario 5. This scenario is the same as scenarios 3 and 4 except that the fourth place holds less value to each player as a meeting place. But, each of them is neutral in the choice between (a) meeting the other in any of the first three places and (b) going to the fourth place, partly in order to meet and partly in order to 'do his own thing'.

This scenario would satisfy the proposed definition of a coordination problem, with $(R4, C4)$ counting as one of the proper coordination equilibria of equal value. So, even though the fourth place is less desirable as a meeting place than the other three, $(R4, C4)$ satisfies the criterion meant to capture the notion of being an equally desirable coordination point. To some extent the problem remains regardless of whether we use Lewis's definition or the proposed one. For it seems odd to allow an outcome to count in the solution of a coordination problem if its desirability to the players *qua* coordination is far less than the other coordination points (and also less than the desirability to the players of going to the fourth place separately *qua* meeting their separate goals). We will see presently that this is not as much of a problem as it seems to be. In any case, the criterion requiring that potential solutions to coordination problems be equally desirable will not solve the problem that prompted its introduction.

Not only does this proposal *not* solve the above problem, it creates new ones as well. For example, suppose two people intentionally go somewhere expressly in order to meet each other. We don't want to say that they actually failed to coordinate because there was someplace else where both of them would have preferred to meet. Under the proposal, however, this is what we would be forced to conclude.

The preceding should tell us that solutions to coordination problems need not all be equally good, even *qua* solutions. How do disparities between equilibria affect the calculation of solutions? One possible answer is to simply calculate expected values based on the probabilities attached to the behavior one anticipates on the part of others. For example, consider the following payoff matrix.

	$C1$	$C2$
$R1$	2 2	0 0
$R2$	1 1	4 4

Let's try to determine Row's best strategy. If he is eighty percent confident that Column will play $C1$ and twenty percent confident that Column will play $C2$, then the expected value of playing $R1$ for him is $.8 \times 2 = 1.6$ while that of playing $R2$ is $.8 \times 1 + .2 \times 4 = 1.6$. So, if his confidence that Column will play $C1$ is greater than eighty percent he should play $R1$ and if it is less than eighty percent he should play $R2$.

Lewis advocates following such reasoning (pp. 25–ff.), but there are a number of problems with it. First, there are certain standard problems. We are basically calculating probabilities here. So, there is the standard question of how to make sense of atomic probabilities (i.e., the probability of an outcome taken in isolation rather than as a frequency distribution). Also, there is the epistemic problem of how one would ascertain these probabilities, even assuming they make sense. We can safely assume that these are not problems for Lewis: this reasoning is only meant to provide a sufficient degree of confidence to give one "decisive reason to do his part" in achieving a particular coordination. Thus, if these probabilities make no sense or are impossible to determine, then they would not provide sufficient reason. If they can be meaningfully determined, then they do.

These standard issues aside, the above cited reasoning raises a possible conflict within Lewis's characterization of coordination. For this is just a case of the kind of reasoning that he rejected as trivial earlier, i.e., reasoning where "the nature of the situation is clear enough so that everybody makes the best choice given his expectations, everybody expects everybody else to make the best choice given his expectations, and so on" (p. 16). Following this type of reasoning the players are merely interested in maximizing their own expected payoffs. The fact that there is a preexisting game involving multiple proper coordination equilibria is irrelevant. The players could follow the same reasoning to determine their best strategies whether the game constituted a coordination problem (by Lewis's definition) or not.

It might seem that Lewis is not actually recommending that players follow this course of reasoning. The degree of confidence one must have in an opposing player's strategy sufficient for one to play the coordinating strategy to match it is simply "a measure of the difficulty of achieving coordination there, [i.e., at that outcome] since however the concordant expectations are produced, weaker expectations will be produced more easily than strong ones" (pp. 26–27). So, a player may simply be gauging the difficulty of coordinating on a particular outcome. But, players are assumed to be rational and to act according to their best interests. Thus, if the difficulty of achieving a particular coordination is too high —i.e., the expected value of the outcome for a given player is too low— then Lewis expects that player to not do his part in achieving that coordination.

> Imagine that a millionaire offers to distribute his fortune equally among a thousand men if each sends him $10; if even one does not, the

millionaire will keep whatever he is sent. I take it that no matter what the thousand do to increase their mutual confidence, it is a practical certainty that the millionaire will not have to pay up. So if I am one of the thousand, I will keep my $10. (p. 27)

The solution to this apparent problem lies in recognizing that in our example above involving the payoff matrix

	$C1$	$C2$
$R1$	2 2	0 0
$R2$	1 1	4 4

we have actually described two games rather than one. And, one game is a coordination problem while the other involves the trivial reasoning about which we were concerned. On the one hand we have the game with no probabilities attached to the other player's strategies. On the other hand we have the game with probabilities attached in which it is always clear what a player should do to satisfy his own interest, whether or not this happens to satisfy the other player's interest. In short, the game with only pure strategies is a coordination problem. Once we introduce numerically determinate expectations, the mathematical affect is to produce a different game. One moral to this story is that the expectations that players have about each other seems to play a large role in determining what counts as a coordination problem and what counts as a solution. Our discussion of the structure of these expectations begins in the next chapter.

3

Conventions

We have seen that the expectations that one player may have about the chances of another playing particular strategies can affect what they do. But, things are still more complicated than that. For, what a player thinks other players expect about what he will do can be significant. And, what he expects them to expect him to expect about what they will do can be significant. And so on. To see this, consider the following example:

Suppose Row and Column would like to meet for dinner tonight. By previous agreement or convention, there are two places they might go: Fat Slice and Moosewood. Let $R1$ represent Row's going to Fat Slice and $R2$ represent Row's going to Moosewood. Similarly, $C1$ represents Column's going to Fat Slice, and $C2$ represents Column's going to Moosewood. Assuming that neither of them has any other interest in going to these places besides meeting, (after possible rescaling) their preferences can be represented by a very simple payoff matrix.

	$C1$	$C2$
$R1$	1 \ 1	0 \ 0
$R2$	0 \ 0	1 \ 1

Even if we assume that they can each attach probabilities to the other's strategies, this is not enough to capture the potential subtleties of mutual expectation that may arise. Suppose that Row and Column agree to meet at Fat Slice. Suppose also that Column incorrectly hears from a third party that Row has for some reason decided to go to Moosewood instead. He scribbles a reminder to himself to see if Row is going to Fat Slice or Moosewood. He checks with Row's secretary who assures him that Row is still planning on going Fat Slice. Later that day Row comes by to see Column, who is out. He sees the reminder on Column's desk. At this point Row intends to go to Fat Slice, Column intends to go to Fat Slice, and they each expect the other to go to Fat Slice. But, Row doubts that Column expects him to go to Fat Slice. Depending on the depth of his doubt and the significance he places on the degree of mutual concordance they share, Row may alter his decision. Thus, the lower order expectation of meeting someplace may depend on a higher order expectation about another's expectations. Both players have first order expectations about going to Fat Slice and about the other player going to Fat Slice. But, Row lacks a second order expectation: he does not expect Column to expect him to go to Fat Slice. In this context we may note along with Lewis that

> The more orders of expectation about action contribute to an agent's decision, the more independent justifications the agent will have; and insofar as he is aware of those justifications, the more firmly his choice is determined. Circumstances that will help to solve a coordination problem, therefore, are circumstances in which the agents become justified in forming mutual expectations belonging to a concordant system. And the more orders, the better. (p. 33)

We will explore these issues more fully beginning in chapter 4, where we discuss common knowledge. For our present purposes we simply assume that, whatever common knowledge is, it is sufficient to guarantee the orders of expectation required for convention.

3.1 Convention Defined and Refined

We could go into much more detail in setting out the motivations behind what Lewis ultimately ends up calling 'convention'. But, we now have enough basic machinery and motivation to comprehensibly state a definition. Lewis's first definition (p. 42) does not require any common knowledge. Since we have already given some motivation for the role of common knowledge in convention, we begin with his first revision. We then state his successive revisions of this, with only minimal intervening motivational explanations.

> A regularity R in the behavior of members of a population P when they are agents in a recurrent situation S is a **convention** if and only

if it is true that, and it is common knowledge in P that, in any instance of S among the members of P,

1. everyone conforms to R;
2. everyone expects everyone else to conform to R;
3. everyone prefers to conform to R on condition that the others do, since S is a coordination problem and uniform conformity to R is a proper coordination equilibrium in S. (p. 58)

This definition works for our basic example of people meeting each other at a standard place because they have succeeded in meeting each other at that place repeatedly in the past. However, there are some forms of conventional behavior for which this definition is not adequate. Lewis gives us the following example:

> If we are contented oligopolists who want to maintain a uniform but fluctuating price for our commodity, we dare not make any explicit agreement on prices; that would be a conspiracy in restraint of trade. But we can come to a tacit understanding—that is, a convention—by our ways of responding to each others' prices. We might, for instance, start to follow a price leader: one firm that takes the initiative in changing prices, with due care to set a price in the range that is satisfactory to all of us. (p. 46)

The problem with applying the above definition to this example is that it seems artificial to carve the behavior up into separate coordination problems. And, to treat it as a long term coordination problem where all contingencies over a long period are part of a single strategy seems a misrepresentation.

Lewis's solution is to devise new criteria that imply the above criteria when we are dealing with distinct coordination problems, but that apply to situations like the one just cited as well. Specifically, he replaces 3 in the above with the following.

3. everyone has approximately the same preferences regarding all possible combinations of actions;
4. everyone prefers that everyone conform to R, on condition that at least all but one conform to R;
5. everyone would prefer that everyone conform to R', on condition that at least all but one conform to R',
   where R' is some possible regularity in the behavior of members of P in S, such that no one in any instance of S among members of P could conform both to R' and to R. (p. 76)

For situations which can described as separate coordination problems these criteria have roughly the following significance: Criterion 4 is meant to insure that R is a coordination equilibrium. Criterion

3, together with 4, is meant to insure that R is a *proper* coordination equilibrium. And, criterion 5 is meant to guarantee that we have a true coordination problem, since R is not unique in being a proper coordination equilibrium.

We are still not quite done with the definition. For, according to this definition, in a population of a million in which everyone conventionally drives on the right side of the road, one deviant driving on the left is sufficient to make this not conventional behavior. To allow for minor deviations from generally conventional behavior, the definition is (finally) revised as follows:

> A regularity R in the behavior of members of a population P when they are agents in a recurrent situation S is a **convention** if and only if it is true that, and it is common knowledge in P that, in almost any instance of S among the members of P,
> 1. almost everyone conforms to R;
> 2. almost everyone expects almost everyone else to conform to R;
> 3. almost everyone has approximately the same preferences regarding all possible combinations of actions;
> 4. almost everyone prefers that any one more conform to R, on condition that almost everyone conform to R;
> 5. everyone would prefer that any one more conform to R', on condition that almost everyone conform to R',
>
> where R' is some possible regularity in the behavior of members of P in S, such that almost no one in almost any instance of S among members of P could conform both to R' and to R. (p. 78)

Certainly Lewis is right in not allowing minor deviations from conventions or major ones in minor percentages of the population to count against those conventions being conventions. But, let us go back and examine his motivation for replacing the characterization in terms of coordination problems with criteria 3 through 5 in the final definition. This was supposedly because some conventions could not be reasonably represented as coordination problems. Since the revised definition encompasses all the sample conventions he presents to us, we might just accept it. However, in doing so we give up the fundamentally game-theoretic explication of convention, together with all the intuitive, technical, and theoretical understanding that has been developed in connection to game theory. Thus, we should explore whether such a revision is truly necessary or whether the problem more properly lies with Lewis's representation of his motivating examples. In the following section we see if we can maintain the flexibility of his broader definition within the bounds of properly described coordination equilibria.

3.2 Convention With and Without Games

Let's return to his example of the contented oligopolists who set prices without explicit agreement. He says that they "can come to a tacit understanding—that is, a convention—by [their] ways of responding to each other's prices" (p. 46). But, what specifically is the convention here. We can't simply respond that there is no one convention, which is why we were forced to modify the definition. For, even the modified definition recognizes distinct "regularities". What might these regularities be? Unfortunately, like Quine with respect to 'convention' before him, Lewis nowhere gives us a definition. However, possibly unlike Quine, this omission may be intentional.

Lewis introduces the term 'regularity' in the context of a discussion of convention (pp. 36–ff.) which notes early on that no two instances of a coordination problem can truly be the same problem. This leads to an analysis of analogy, precedence, salience, etc., that is meant in part to illustrate the difficulty of explaining what is *regular* about a regularity. Rather than drag through the vast literature on sameness, similarity, etc., we will accept that this is a difficult and *separate* problem from the one at hand. Thus, we allow for an intuitive understanding of 'regularity' within conventional parameters.

So, how about our oligopolists? Lewis does give us an example of the type of regularity that might apply: they could "follow a price leader: one firm that takes the initiative in changing prices, with due care to set a price in the range that is satisfactory to all of [them]." The problem is that prices can be changed at any time.

> How long is a coordination problem? Pretend, already idealizing, that we set our prices every morning and cannot change them later in the day. Then each business day is a coordination problem. But a day is too short. Our customers take more than a day to shop around; they compare my price for today with yours for yesterday and someone else's for tomorrow. We are leaving out most of the coordination: coordination of one's action on one day with another's action on another nearby day. If, on the other hand, we take longer stretches as the coordination problems, then —contrary to the definition—everyone has time for several different choices within a single coordination problem. We might pretend that everyone starts each week by choosing a contingency plan specifying what to do in every possible circumstance during the week (a *strategy* in the sense of the theory of games), and then follows his plan all week without making any further choice. Then a business week is a coordination problem in which everyone makes only his initial contingency plan. But this treatment badly misdescribes what we do; and it still leaves out the coordination between, say, my prices for Friday

and yours for next Monday. (pp. 46–47)

According to Lewis the coordination characterization gives sufficient but not necessary conditions for a convention. The problem is that it may be difficult (or impossible) to precisely state the coordination problems in which a convention arises. His later account does not suffer from this problem since it does not require that we give self-contained coordination problems.

Clearly Lewis is right in claiming that we cannot accurately present the contented oligopolists example in terms of the coordination problems he describes. But, has he given the only possible presentation in terms of coordination problems? Why does he insist that coordination problems be self-contained, but not that "recurrent situations" in which regularities arise be self-contained? Could we not give some other coordination problems that would accurately depict the contented oligopolists? We now describe such a coordination problem.

Recall that a coordination problem is a situation "of interdependent decision by two or more agents in which coincidence of interest predominates and in which there are two or more proper coordination equilibria" (p. 24). For the oligopolists the situation is one where they want to maintain a uniform but fluctuating price without making any explicit agreements. In order for there to be a convention, there must be alternative ways they might do this about which they are all relatively neutral in the way we described earlier. In other words, these alternatives must be coordination equilibria (for each of them nobody would have been better off had any one agent acted differently), and they must be *proper* coordination equilibria (each agent strictly prefers it to any result he could attain given the others' choices). What might some of the alternatives be? Lewis offers us one:

1. Follow a price leader, one firm that takes the initiative in changing prices, with due care to set a price in the range that is satisfactory to all of them.

It is unclear here whether the initiative to change prices is always left up to the same firm or to whichever firm happens to seize it. Let us assume the former. Then, if there are, e.g., five firms that might serve as price leader, there are four alternatives to that firm being price leader. But there are other alternatives as well, one of which we have already mentioned:

6. Follow a price leader, whichever firm currently happens to take the initiative in changing prices. If more than one seems to take the initiative at the same time, follow, e.g., the one with the

highest price.

Here are a still others:

7. Rotate the setting of the price about the group in some order, e.g., alphabetical by firm name.
8. Two firms act as price leaders, they each choose a price and everyone else chooses a price somewhere between the two.
9. All of the firms set a price at the beginning of a week (month or whatever seems reasonable). They then reset prices as often as seems normal such that all subsequent prices are within some ϵ of the average at the beginning of the week. Initial prices the following week are no more than, e.g., half of a standard deviation (of the preceding week's closing prices) from the high or low firm's closing price the preceding week.
10. All firms change their prices regularly, and all firms check prices when they are about to change their price. If their current price is below the current average, they must raise it. If it is above average, they can do as they wish.

Obviously we could come up with many more of these. Some of these might not be very feasible, but neither is a contented oligopoly with no explicit communication. Even with communication it is problematic; consider OPEC. In any case, some of these alternatives are perfectly believable. And, Lewis's revised definition depends on the existence of some of them as much as his original does. The revised definition requires an alternative regularity, R', just as the original requires two proper coordination equilibria. For the sake of simplicity, let's consider an oligopoly of five firms, A, B, C, D, and E, with a convention in which A sets the price, and the others follow. There is also nothing to prevent us from assuming that the five conventions (one for each firm setting the price) satisfy the criteria for proper coordination equilibria, viz: each firm finds such an outcome at least as acceptable as any alternative in which all but one follow the convention, and each one strictly prefers this to anything he could achieve assuming all the others conform.

Someone who feels that Lewis's revision is necessary might point out that we haven't yet given alternative strategies simply by saying follow A, follow B, etc. for each of them. We want to know, e.g., if A raises his price by five dollars today, what is each of the others going to do and when. And, how will they each respond to what the others do when A raises his price by five dollars? And so on. If we could give these strategies, then we would have indeed described a game. But, it would not be the coordination game that the oligopoly is playing.

Asking us to describe such games is asking us to describe irrelevancies. We no more need do this than we need describe how fast Jennifer walks when she is on her way to meet her husband at the conventional time at the conventional restaurant. Again, this criticism applies just as well to the revised definition as to the original. We have already countenanced a notion of 'regularity' that is broad enough to deal with intuitive examples that are reasonably clear. We should permit similar latitude in the specification of strategies in a coordination game.

Even if we permit such strategies as *B follows A's lead in setting a price.*, there is still a problem with the original definition that is solved in the revised account. We have specified the strategies that yield coordination equilibria, but we have said nothing about other strategies that might be played. We have described alternative ways the players might coordinate, but we have not described alternatives to coordination. This problem does not arise in the revised definition because it does not require that we give non-regularities: the only alternatives to regularities that we need specify are other regularities. Regardless of how seriously we take it, however, this is not a genuine problem.

In the first place, we have given alternatives to coordination. One obvious example is where no one takes the lead and where A follows B, B follows C, C follows D, D follows E, and E follows A. This could lead to a varying price where at most five prices are rotated around. Thus, they achieve fluctuation but not uniformity. Besides, the pattern would be so obvious that they would be caught conspiring anyway: hardly a 'coordination'. Alternatively, and no doubt worse, this could lead to the price fixing on a single value.

Perhaps it seems that examples like this are not genuine alternatives, alternatives such as setting the price according to the firm's perception of the market, or setting the price so as to eliminate the weakest of the other four. If we know that the attainment of a convention is intended then, we need not accept a request for such alternatives. It is unreasonable since it amounts to a request that we find (more than one) coordination equilibrium in a game of conflict. While it is sometimes possible to find these, we are interested in games that are essentially cooperative. However, if the goal is to determine whether convention can be attained under certain circumstances, then we may have to consider a request for such alternatives after all.

Such a request plays against the revised definition as well as the original since it is stipulated that almost everyone has approximately the same preferences with regard to all possible combinations of actions. If such alternatives are to interfere with the possibility of coordination because some players would rather do well on their own or at the expense of others than cooperate, then it will interfere with the possibility of achieving a convention according to the revised definition because preferences will not approximately coincide. The same point holds for all the criteria for convention. As Lewis points out, if a situation S "is a self-contained problem of interdependent decision, in which each agent involved makes one choice of action and the outcome of each depends on the actions of all [i.e., a game] ... *then S is a coordination problem and uniform conformity to R is a coordination equilibrium*" (pp. 68–69). Thus, within the confines of a stated game, any outcome that satisfies the revised definition of a convention will satisfy the original.

Perhaps one might simply be concerned that such alternatives should be represented even though they are not suspected of playing any convention killing role. In other words, it is assumed that they play no role at all in the possibility or impossibility of achieving a convention. In that case they can all be grouped under the strategy *Do anything else.* for each player. We appear to be back in a situation where any other details of following the action are irrelevant. It might seem that this should not count as a legitimate strategy because no specific action at any level of detail is given. In this sense such a move is different from, e.g., failing to specify the speed with which someone walks to a restaurant. It is also true that we cannot appeal to Lewis's maneuver of allowing disjunctions of strategies (p. 23) since this involved only finite disjunctions of explicitly given alternative strategies. We might accept these objections as showing that we have not completely specified the game under the ordinary understanding of representing, at least on some level, all the possible actions. Still, there is no reason for us to limit ourselves to that understanding. We can accept that all alternative courses have not been intuitively given. But, this does not prevent us from having a strategy in the formal structure as a catchall for the representation of all irrelevant alternatives. Given this, it is difficult to see what harm there is in simply not referring to those alternatives at all.

In this chapter we have looked at Lewis's game-theoretic approach to convention via coordination equilibria. We found it to be a fruitful way to look at convention, indeed more fruitful than Lewis himself found it. He thought it necessary to abandon this approach to achieve a fully general characterization. We have seen that it is not necessary to do so. Below, in chapter 10, we will see that it is possible to make the account even more fully game-theoretic. One basic aspect of the characterization that we merely touched on above is the mutual expectations necessary between participants in a convention. This is a main subject of the next chapter.

4

Common Knowledge and Coordination

In the beginning of the last chapter we briefly discussed the significance of the expectations that participants in a convention hold about themselves and each other. In fact in defining 'convention' we required that the relevant intentions and actions of (almost) all participants be common knowledge amongst them. However, we did not say what common knowledge is. In this chapter we will more fully examine these mutual expectations and the common knowledge that underlies them.

4.1 The Structure of Mutual Expectations

We have already seen that convention involves not just a participant's expectation about other participants' behavior but also their expectations about his (and each other's) expectations. In fact there is no reason to stop there; we must consider expectations of expectations of expectations, and expectations of expectations of expectations of expectations, etc. To facilitate this discussion we adopt Lewis's recursive definition of an nth-**order expectation**:

> A first-order expectation about something is an ordinary expectation about it.
> An $(n+1)^{\text{th}}$-order expectation about something ($n \geq 1$) is an ordinary expectation about someone else's n^{th}-order expectation about it. (p. 28)

Let us focus on a convention between just two people, you and me. What desires and expectations are necessary in order for me to desire to conform to the convention (and presumably follow through on my desire)?[6] We need two premises:

1. I desire that I conform on the condition that you will conform.
2. I expect that you will conform.

Premise 2 gives us a first-order expectation. What reason do I have to believe this? Presumably I have replicated for myself some of the reasoning that I think you will go through in this coordination. This yields two further premises:

3. I expect that you desire that you conform on the condition that I will conform.
4. I expect that you expect that I will conform.

The second-order expectation given in premise 4 is supported by two further premises:

5. I expect that you expect that I desire that I conform on the condition that you will conform.
6. I expect that you expect that I expect that you will conform.

Obviously this chain of expectations and desires can get quite complicated very quickly, and working through the layers rapidly becomes dizzying. (Actually, it is even worse than it might seem from this representation. I have said nothing about the justification for the odd-numbered expectations; the chain is not a chain but a tree.) Because of this Lewis sets things out in terms of *reasons* for expectations, which then yield expectations provided that the relevant ancillary premises about degree of rationality are met. Thus, for example, in place of statements 4 and 5 Lewis has one that says I have reason to expect that you have reason to expect that I have reason to desire that I conform. He then tacks on an assumption that I expect that you expect that I am rational to the degree necessary for this reason to fire—i.e. for me to infer based on it.

> So if I somehow happen to have an nth-order expectation about the action in this two-person coordination problem, I may work my way outward [i.e. down the chain of premises] ... to lower- and lower-order expectations about action. Provided that I go on long enough, and provided all the needed higher-order expectations about preferences and rationality are available, I eventually come out with a first-order expectation about your action—which is what I need in order to know how I should act. (p. 31)

---

[6]The following closely follows Lewis's analysis (pp. 28–ff.), but there are some differences.

The important question that remains is how one can "somehow happen to have an nth-order expectation". If lower-order expectations are dependent on higher-order expectations, then how can we ever coordinate our actions that depend on these expectations? We will see below that in situations sufficient for common knowledge to arise there are enough orders of expectation to underlie coordination.

Common Knowledge is a notion which has proven useful in a variety of contexts over the last few decades. Despite a lot of valuable research in characterizing the idea, there is still confusion over when it is generally applicable. Barwise (1989a) gives one of the most complete theoretical analyses of the various approaches to common knowledge and how they relate to each other. In the conclusion of that paper Barwise looks at three distinct basic questions: (i) What is the correct analysis of common knowledge? (ii) Where does it come from? (iii) How is it used? He proposes answers to the first two questions but, in effect, a rejection of the third. He says, "My own guess is that common knowledge per se ... is not actually all that useful. It is a necessary but not sufficient condition for action." (p. 219). Barwise's view is in accord with Lewis's characterization, in which the ancillary assumptions about rationality are what allow us to use our common knowledge. One of the primary goals of this and the next two chapters is to give an explication of common knowledge that will show that it is indeed useful. Barwise continues, "What suffices for common knowledge to be useful is that it arise in some fairly straightforward [easily perceived] shared situation." We will find ourselves in agreement with the spirit of Barwise's analysis. We will differ primarily by taking the perception of the situation to be part of the common knowledge itself, thus making common knowledge sufficient for action (or at least intention to act).

The relations between knowledge, common knowledge, shared situations, coordinated actions, etc. are complex, and it is easy to get them confused. An example from the beginning of that same paper (p. 201) serves as a good illustration.

Suppose James and Eleri are playing poker, and each of them is dealt an ace. Each of them thus knows that at least one of them has an ace. Suppose Jennifer now comes up and asks, "Do either of you know whether the other one has an ace?" They can both truthfully answer "no". But, suppose she should say, "At least one of you has an ace. Now do you know whether the other has an ace?" If they answer simultaneously, they should both still say "no"; however, upon hearing each other say "no" they can each easily conclude that the other must have an ace. For, assuming honesty, a player with no ace would have to say "yes" once given the information that at least one of them has an ace.

What is apparently paradoxical about this is that each of them already had that information. So, how can it have been added by Jennifer?[7] Barwise answers that by announcing it publicly, she made what was previously knowledge private to each of them *common knowledge*. This answer is slightly deceptive. It is deceptive because, issues concerning their cognitive abilities aside, James and Eleri do attain common knowledge here when Jennifer makes her announcement. But, common knowledge is not necessary to explain their understanding of each other's answers; second-order knowledge is all that is needed.

That they have common knowledge that at least one of them has an ace should be self-evident and will be justified by all the characterizations of common knowledge given below. That they need only second-order knowledge will be defended in the next section.

In the next section we will review the three basic approaches that have been taken to common knowledge. Following that I will examine a classic coordinated action problem from the distributed computing literature, viz the coordinated attack, or two generals problem. It is 'common knowledge' that this problem is easily proven to be unsolvable—i.e. it is impossible to coordinate the action. I will show that under the circumstances set out in the problem it is possible to coordinate the action. I will then use this example to further analyze the relation between coordinated action and common knowledge.

4.2 Common Knowledge

The Iterated Approach

The iterated approach to common knowledge is probably the first one to suggest itself upon recognizing that there is more to common knowledge that φ than simply the knowledge that φ on the part of all the relevant agents. To simplify our discussion we will consider a case of just two agents, A and B having common knowledge of one proposition, φ.

On the iterated approach, we say that A and B have common knowledge that φ, provided that:

1. A knows φ.
   B knows φ.
2. A knows that B knows φ.
   B knows that A knows φ.

---

[7]Barwise calls this "the famous Conway paradox". For more details cf. van Emde Boas et al. 1981.

3. A knows that B knows that A knows φ.
   B knows that A knows that B knows φ.

$\vdots$

The iterated approach is probably the easiest one to understand, at least in terms of traditional formalisms. Though not finitely representable therein, the iterated approach can be set out in ordinary epistemic logic. Both of the others allow a finite representation of common knowledge, but they involve using some sort of nonwellfounded structure. The iterated approach has been widely studied in the context of distributed computing. (Cf. Halpern 1987, Halpern and Moses 1990. Fagin et al. 1995 subsumes these and gives a comprehensive treatment of the epistemic work by its authors.)

Mindful of the iterated approach, we now explain why common knowledge is not necessary to account for what is said by James and Eleri in the card playing situation. If we let 'At least one of James and Eleri has an ace.' stand for φ in the definition above, we can see that they need proceed no further than the second entry in the list to be able to infer that the other has an ace. To illustrate this let us consider a situation in which they can each make the inference but in which common knowledge does not arise. Suppose that the scenario is as before except that Jennifer talks to each of them separately as follows. Assume she talks to James first. Now, unbeknownst to James, Eleri can hear their entire conversation. Thus, Eleri hears Jennifer ask, "Given that at least one of you has an ace, do you know whether James has an ace?" And, she hears James answer "no". Similarly, James overhears her conversation with Eleri. In this situation, according to any of the approaches to common knowledge described herein, they do not have common knowledge that at least one of them has an ace. Nonetheless, they are each able to conclude that the other has an ace.

This is not to say that they do not have common knowledge of φ. They do. And, they got it when Jennifer made her announcement in front of them. Ignoring questions about their cognitive abilities (or degrees of rationality, to follow Lewis), it should be clear that in this situation they have the knowledge attributed to them on all levels of the iterated hierarchy.

We now have the beginnings of an answer to the question of how one can "somehow happen to have an nth-order expectation". In the example we have been looking at there is no attempt to coordinate an action. But, we can see how, on the iterated account, the second-order knowledge that the children needed to infer as they did follows from their possession of common knowledge. This is far from a complete answer. We still have not explained how the infinite hierarchy arises or is justified.

The Fixed-Point Approach

As we just noted, a problem with the iterated approach is that it forces an infinite representation of common knowledge. But, this is not just a representational issue. There may be debate over the potential infinity of our knowledge capacity, but there is little question about the finiteness of the actual knowledge of any finite agent. Nobody actually knows infinitely many things in practice, but this seems to be exactly what is required of anyone who has common knowledge of anything at all.[8] One possible way to capture our intuitions about common knowledge in a finite representation is to allow self reference. If we let τ represent the fact that φ is common knowledge for A and B, then we can represent τ itself by

A and B know (φ and τ)

This is the approach advocated by Harman (1977). Not only is this account finitely expressible, but it is also stronger than the iterated account. On the iterated approach knowledge is of course iterated, but common knowledge is not. Harman points out that "the self-referential formulation ... has the consequence that, where there is mutual knowledge, it is known that there is mutual knowledge" (p. 423). Putting things in our terminology, according to the fixed-point approach, common knowledge that φ is itself common knowledge; however, in order to represent this on the iterated approach we would need an infinite sequence of infinite sequences of sentences. And, the existence of the first infinite sequence does not imply the existence of the others. In certain distributed computing applications, this property of common knowledge is essential for a variety of results (Halpern and Moses 1990, pp. 572–ff.). For the basic notion as applied to ordinary human understanding this does seem to be a reasonable feature of common knowledge: how could people have common knowledge of φ and not be mutually aware of their common knowledge? Nonetheless, it may not be immediately obvious what is lost in the iterated account beyond our ability to express this.[9] We will return to this point below.

---

[8] My comments will generally be phrased as about human possessors of knowledge and human agents. Most of them will carry over *mutatis mutandis* to computer processes.

[9] Citing early work of McCarthy, Barwise says that "common knowledge of σ should entail common knowledge of common knowledge that σ" (p. 203). Perhaps this is explained by McCarthy, but if so, Barwise does not present the explanation.

It seems that the fixed-point approach solves the problem of needing to appeal to the infinite when representing common knowledge. But before accepting this, we should consider a point raised by Clark and Marshall (1981). They studied common knowledge (or mutual knowledge, as they call it) in connection with how we can make meaningful uses of definite reference.

They point out that the iterated approach seems to yield a paradox. Given that definite reference requires mutual knowledge and that each of the infinity of necessary conditions requires a finite (albeit small) time to check, it would seem that to even attempt a felicitous use of definite reference would require an infinite amount of time. But, definite reference is ordinarily made in a finite amount of time, on the order of a few seconds. They also point out that Harman's fixed-point approach will not resolve the paradox even though it manages to finitely represent common knowledge. The fixed-point approach says that: A and B have common knowledge that $\varphi =_{df}$.

(τ) A and B know (φ and τ)

In order to make a felicitous definite reference A must assure herself that she and B have common knowledge of the reference—i.e. that φ. In order to do this she must check that τ; so, she must check that she and B know φ and τ. But, in order to do that she must check that she and B know that she and B know φ and τ. Etc. "So just the fact that mutual knowledge can be captured in a single statement doesn't absolve Ann and Bob [A and B] from checking each of an infinity of statements. Although the representation *looks* simpler, its assessment isn't necessarily simpler." (Clark and Marshall 1981, p. 17)

How then is common knowledge to be finitely established? That is, how can one verify an infinity of conditions in a finite amount of time on the basis of finite evidence? The answer in a nutshell is shared situations.

The Shared-Situation Approach

This is the approach advocated by Barwise and by Lewis and Clark & Marshall before him. It too trades infinite expression for self reference. But, unlike either the fixed-point or the iterated approach, it does not give an explicit statement of what common knowledge is, rather it describes a situation the existence of which is necessary and sufficient for common knowledge to arise. There is thus a uniqueness in the two prior accounts that is missing in this one. For, there may be more than

---

(The reference that Barwise gives for McCarthy et al. 1977, is not published in those proceedings.)

one situation giving rise to common knowledge of the same fact.[10] On this account, A and B have common knowledge that φ just in case there is a situation s such that:

- $s \models \varphi$
- $s \models A$ knows s.
- $s \models B$ knows s.

Barwise (1989a) develops much of the model theory of situations with respect to common knowledge. In chapters 7, 8, and 9 we will give our own characterization of semantic notions, such as what it means for a sentence to be true in a situation. For the present we simply think of situations intuitively as partial possible worlds. So, $s \models (A$ knows s.) can be viewed as saying that 'A knows s.' is true at s. That is, in situation s, A knows that s is the situation. We will go into more detail about what it means for A to know that s is the situation, but for now we note that intuitively this means at least that A knows anything that is true in s.

This concludes our discussion of the basics of the approaches to common knowledge to date. In the following section we set out a particular problem that will be useful in illustrating important points in our own analysis of common knowledge.

4.3 The Unsolvable Coordinated Attack

A version of the following problem was first described by Gray (1978), who called it the "generals paradox". Since then it has generally been called the coordinated attack problem. (The following version is quoted from Halpern and Moses 1990, pp. 555–6.)

> Two divisions of an army are camped on two hilltops overlooking a common valley. In the valley awaits the enemy. It is clear that if both divisions attack the enemy simultaneously, they will win the battle; whereas if only one division attacks, it will be defeated. The divisions do not initially have plans for launching an attack on the enemy, and the commanding general of the first division wishes to coordinate a simultaneous attack (at some time the next day). Neither general will decide to attack unless he is sure that the other will attack with him. The generals can only communicate by means of a messenger. Normally, it takes the messenger one hour to get from one encampment to the other. However, it is possible that he will get lost in the dark

---

[10]The lack of agreement over the relation between facts, propositions, true propositions, sentences, etc. is well known, cf., e.g., Barwise 1989c. I hope to skirt these issues to the extent possible and hope that the reader will put on my usage the most reasonable face he can, consistent with his own views.

or, worse yet, be captured by the enemy. Fortunately, on this particular night, everything goes smoothly. How long will it take them to coordinate an attack?

The standard claim is that, even if everything does go smoothly, no agreement can ever be reached and thus neither general can ever decide to attack. As Halpern & Moses point out this is a virtual folk theorem of operating systems theory. Here is the argument. Suppose that A sends a message saying "We should attack at dawn." to general B. This is enough for B to know that A wants to attack at dawn.[11] But, B also knows that A can't know that he knows this because the messenger might not have arrived. So, he sends back his own messenger telling A of his receipt of the message and his agreement. To indicate that everything is confirmed A acknowledges receipt of this message by sending a response to B. It might seem that the attack is now coordinated because both A and B know that they each want to attack at dawn. And, each of them knows that they both know this. The problem is that A cannot know that his last message to B ever arrived. Thus, at this point A can only be sure that B knows he sent an initial response to A. From A's perspective, B may not know that A knows that B has agreed to attack at dawn. As long as A has this doubt, he would be foolish to attack at dawn because B might not attack if he didn't get A's last message. It should be clear that this reasoning can be generalized so that no finite number of messages suffices to coordinate the attack. What seems to be going on here is that the generals are adding layers to an iterated knowledge hierarchy like the one in the iterated approach to common knowledge; they add one layer for each pair of messages sent. But, since they can never actually fill up the entire hierarchy of necessary iterations, they can never attain common knowledge of their joint desire to attack at dawn. Thus, they cannot coordinate the attack.

Halpern & Moses even make this slightly more rigorous by giving an argument by mathematical induction "that the generals can never attack and be guaranteed that they are attacking simultaneously" (p. 556). Below we will be looking closely at induction arguments both in connection with generally accepted situations of common knowledge and in connection with this situation. Thus, it is helpful to see what

---

[11]We assume that both A and B are such that if they hold the right attitudes towards what they should do and towards each other's attitudes about it, then each will indeed do it, rather than merely concluding that they should do it. So the result will be coordinated action. Thus, if they obtain common knowledge that they should do something, then they will do it.

they have to say.[12]

We argue by induction on d—the number of messages delivered by the time of the attack—that d messages do not suffice. Clearly, if no message is delivered, then B will not know of the intended attack, and simultaneous attack is impossible. For the inductive step assume that k messages do not suffice. If $k+1$ messages suffice, then the sender of the $(k+1)^{st}$ message attacks without knowing whether his last message arrived. Since whenever one general attacks they both do, the intended receiver of the $(k+1)^{st}$ message must attack regardless of whether the $(k+1)^{st}$ message is delivered. Thus, the $(k+1)^{st}$ message is irrelevant, and k messages suffice, contradicting the inductive hypothesis.

I hasten to state that, while I will argue that the above view of the coordinated attack problem is not entirely correct, there are no technical mistakes in any of the above. The problem is that the view fails to account for all the possibilities.

4.4 A Solution

Let us consider the predicament of the two generals exactly as above; they each follow the usually described procedure up to a point. General A sends to general B a proposed time for a simultaneous attack together with some number n, the number of messages that each of them must receive to be sure that they will both attack as agreed. As described above the problem is that one of them will receive n messages before the other, and he won't be able to tell whether or not the other received the last message. And, receipt of that last message is necessary for the attack to be successfully coordinated. Nevertheless, in this case A proposes in the initial message that they agree to the following procedure. When the last of them receives his n^{th} message, he sends a response anyway. The recipient of this message sends a response as well, and they both continue to do so as long as they are successful until just before the agreed upon attack time. At this point they are each to reason thus. *I don't know how many messages I've received. But, it was well more than enough to be sure that each of us got n of them, and for each of us to know that and for each of us to know that we know it, and so on as far as I'm willing to consider. So, we both have more than enough assurance to believe that the other will attack. So, I will attack.* Recall that the original description prescribes that on this occasion all messages go through smoothly. So, on this occasion they both do exactly as just proposed, thus successfully coordinating the attack.

---

[12] Any perceived similarity of the following to the argument of the *sorites* paradox should be viewed as portentous.

The first question of course is: How is this possible? Isn't this just a cheat, like the two people in chapter 2 who happened to serendipitously meet at Saint Patrick's Cathedral in New York by making incorrect assumptions? Perhaps. But, unlike the two people meeting in New York, the generals agreed to make those 'incorrect' assumptions together. (One might raise the issue of whether or not we have sufficient conditions for them to agree to this procedure. We actually do. But, to cut down on confusion we can stipulate that it was agreed upon face to face, prior to the current situation.) Still, can we make any rigorous sense of the above, and can we explain how this solution is possible given the correctness of standard reasoning?

5

Conventional Knowledge and Belief

The astute reader will have noticed that we did not in the last chapter distinguish between justified belief and knowledge. Indeed, we said little about belief at all. One reason for this is consistency with the previous literature we have been discussing, most notably Lewis 1969. We have noted that Lewis gives a shared situation definition of common knowledge. Explicitly, he says on p. 56,

> Let us say that it is *common knowledge* in a population P that ____ if and only if some state of affairs s holds such that:
> (1) Everyone in P has reason to believe that s holds.
> (2) s indicates to everyone in P that everyone in P has reason to believe that s holds.
> (3) s indicates to everyone in P that ____ .

Thus, for Lewis, common knowledge is defined in terms of belief. Barwise (1989a) mentions mutual belief as a "relative" of common knowledge, but never says anything about it. He does say a bit about the relation between common knowledge and another relative, shared information. We will return to that issue below. And, he does not directly say that Lewis's definition is exactly the same as his account; however, before giving his account he does say, "Lewis in fact adopts the shared-situation account presented below as the basic definition." (Barwise 1989a, p. 102). Thus, if he does not fail to make a distinction, it is fair to say that he makes little of any such distinction he might be making. Further examples of this relative indifference can be found in other already cited papers.

5.1 Mutual Belief and Common Knowledge

As a first step in exploring further we give a shared-situation account of mutual belief. Besides being expressed in terms of knowledge rather than belief, an obvious difference of mutual belief from common knowledge is that the object of belief may not be true. How can we reflect this difference? As was noted in section 4.2 A knowing s implies that A knows φ for any φ such that $s \models \varphi$. (This will be an immediate consequence of formal definition of 'A knows s.' in the logic set out in chapter 9.) Thus, it should be clear that the shared-situation account of common knowledge given above is equivalent to the following.

There is a situation s such that:

- $s \models A$ knows φ.
- $s \models B$ knows φ.
- $s \models A$ knows s.
- $s \models B$ knows s.

Our reason for giving this alternative definition is that it leads more naturally into a shared situation account of mutual belief. On the shared situation approach, we can say A and B have *mutual belief* that φ just in case there is a situation s such that:

- $s \models A$ believes φ.
- $s \models B$ believes φ.
- $s \models A$ believes s.
- $s \models B$ believes s.

How well does this reflect Lewis's definition? To answer, we will have to spell out some of his terms a little more. "Let us say that s *indicates* to someone X that ____ if and only if, if X had reason to believe that s held, X would thereby have reason to believe that ____ ."[13] (Lewis 1969, pp. 52–53) Also, recall from section 4.1 that Lewis speaks in terms of reasons to expect (or here believe) so as to avoid the question of which expectations are actually held. These depend on X's "inductive standards and background information". This is more a factor for unpacking shared situations into iterated attributions of belief than for the shared-situation account itself. In any case, if we ignore this aspect and assume that anyone with reason to believe φ believes φ, and that anyone who believes φ has reason to do so, then we can compare the just given shared-situation account of mutual belief with Lewis's definition of common knowledge. In particular, we can ask whether this account implies his definition.

Assume that A and B have mutual belief that φ on the shared-situation account. Then, in s, (1) A and B believe that s holds. And, (2) if A believes s holds, then since $s \models B$ believes s, and $s \models A$ believes s,

---

[13]I have replaced variable names in Lewis's definition above and in this and subsequent quotes to be more consistent with the notation we have been using.

s indicates to A that in s, both A and B believe that s holds. And, similarly for B. Finally, (3) if A believes s holds, then since $s \models A$ believes φ, A believes A believes φ. And, this implies that A believes φ (both intuitively and in many, though not all, standard logics of belief). And, we can similarly show that s indicates to B that φ.

A couple of points about this: First, Lewis's definition requires not just that in s, A and B believe that s holds, but that s holds. Thus, to yield Lewis's definition, we must assume that there is some situation s_0 (or possibly a set of situations) which is designated as reflecting what is actually true, and s must be a subsituation of s_0. At least as significant are the inferences necessary to derive from this shared-situation account of shared belief the third condition in Lewis's definition. The inference from A believes A believes φ to A believes φ is intuitive, but it cannot be derived in a logic without axioms that may be stronger than desired, e.g., **T** (the knowledge axiom) or **5** (negative introspection).[14] In particular, once the **T** axiom (roughly: anything that is believed is true) is added to the logic, it is generally regarded as a logic of knowledge rather than belief. Negative introspection (roughly: if a person doesn't believe something, then she believes that she doesn't believe it) is more typically acceptable as a belief axiom; however, since there are indefinitely many things that any one person does not believe, this would also require indefinitely many things that that person believes. This runs contrary to our basic agenda. We will return to these concerns in chapter 8. Examining which rationality axioms we can jettison or retain while preserving common knowledge is also somewhat contrary to our *bottom up* approach, as we will discuss presently.

What more can we say about Lewis's belief-based common knowledge in terms of shared situations? Neither the shared-situation account of common knowledge nor that of mutual belief directly reflects his definition, even leaving aside the distinction between believing and having reason to believe. However, we can give a definition that more closely reflects Lewis's account. Let us say A and B have *Lewis-common knowledge* that φ just in case there is a true situation s_0 and a subsituation

---

[14]**T** and **5** are historical names for these axioms going back to C.I. Lewis. For more on them and associated logical systems cf. Chellas 1980. For the epistemic reading of these axioms cf. Hintikka 1962 and Fagin et al. 1995.

s of s_0: such that:

(1) $s_0 \models A$ believes s.
$s_0 \models B$ believes s.

(2) For any s', if $s' \models A$ believes s, then $s' \models A$ believes B believes s.
For any s', if $s' \models A$ believes s, then $s' \models A$ believes A believes s.
For any s', if $s' \models B$ believes s, then $s' \models B$ believes A believes s.
For any s', if $s' \models B$ believes s, then $s' \models B$ believes B believes s.

(3) For any s', if $s' \models A$ believes s, then $s' \models A$ believes φ.
For any s', if $s' \models B$ believes s, then $s' \models B$ believes φ.

This definition does not require that in s, A believes that s holds. It might be that s holds, but it is only in some larger situation that A believes that s. For example, in the two generals example, once each of them has sent four messages, they will each believe that each of them has sent three messages. Of course that situation will not satisfy the other clauses of this account. Let us assume that $s_0 = s$ here. In that case clause (2) becomes effectively redundant, and this reduces to mutual belief, rather than common knowledge, according to the shared situation accounts given above.

There is a shared-situation account of common knowledge expressible in terms of belief, obtained by simply replacing 'knows' with 'believes' in the original definition from Barwise given in section 4.2:

A and B have common knowledge that φ just in case there is a situation s such that:

- $s \models \varphi$
- $s \models A$ believes s.
- $s \models B$ believes s.

The only beliefs in the account are ones about which the believers cannot possibly be mistaken. So, this is intuitively equivalent to the knowledge-based definition. Also, for any logic in which knowledge and belief are distinguished by the presence or absence, respectively, of the **T** axiom, the two are equivalent.

We might assume that this is the account that Lewis had in mind and that other authors assumed him to have meant, but it is not necessary to attribute so straightforward an error. Something more subtle is going on.

5.2 The Ups and Downs of Mutual Understanding

Like previous authors, we will ultimately find little of significance for our purposes in the distinction between belief-based and knowledge-based *mutual understanding* (my attempt at a neutral term). Of course for other purposes the distinction between knowledge and even justified belief may be significant, or at least controversial (Moser 1986). And, even for some of the facts about which there is common knowledge, this may be an important distinction. Even if our concerns have little need of such distinctions, the relation between common knowledge and mutual belief has previously been extensively studied. For example, Bonanno and Nehring (2000) explored various properties; in particular, properties sufficient for these to coincide in some standard epistemic logics.

Views from the Top

Authors going back at least to Aumann (1976) have noted that mutual understanding of rationality is both apparently necessary and apparently a problem for agents to interact in competitive situations. (Cf., e.g., Lismont and Mongin 1994; Stalnaker 1994, 1996; Stuart 1997; Lismont and Mongin 2000; Bonanno and Nehring 2000.) Problems include how a rational agent can respond when a competitor does something "irrational", how people could even be irrational, how people could be logically omniscient—as would appear to be necessary, etc. (On this last one we will say more in chapter 8.) One goal of such work is to "weaken the agents' cognitive abilities, but retain the standard assumption that the rules of the game are common belief among the players" (Lismont and Mongin 2000, p. 22). In this work cognitive abilities are weakened so that basic logical omniscience is eliminated: people don't know or believe all logical truths. But, for example, if two formulae are provably equivalent, than belief in them is also provably equivalent. This is so even if one of the formulae is atomic and the other is logically very complex. And, this means that if someone believes even one thing, then he automatically believes indefinitely many equivalent things.

Some common points in the work we have just been citing are that the focus is primarily on competitive rather than collaborative problems and that a top down approach is taken to those problems, one that first seeks to preserve assumptions of rationality and then sees what can be removed while maintaining that. Another way in which this approach is top-down is that it seeks to determine what the logical implications (hence acceptability) are of axioms such as *truth of common belief*— that anything that is mutually believed is true (Bonanno and Nehring 2000). We are viewing things more from the bottom up. How can people build to common knowledge and convention at all? People are capable of knowing at most finitely many, indeed a very few, things, and we are examining how they could come to conventions at all under these circumstances. Since we are exploring convention, we are more focused on problems with a collaborative rather than a competitive focus. This is a complementary rather than a conflicting take on things, just as is taking a bottom-up rather than top-down approach.

Note that Barwise also takes something of a top-down approach, although in a different way. When he defines the satisfaction ($\models$) relation, he does so co-inductively. That is, he defines it to be the largest subclass of a particular class satisfying the requisite conditions. Essentially this means that anything goes in the relation unless there is an inductively defined reason to throw it out. The satisfaction relation that we define in later chapters will be far less inclusive. We leave the specifics until then, although some of the intuitive motivation is given more immediately below, in the next chapter.

Our convention-focused, bottom-up view is more in the spirit of Lewis, but we intend to take it even further. In particular, we are interested in how agents can come to conventions of logic and rationality, as opposed to which axioms of rationality have acceptable implications. Note that, in the logic we set out in chapter 9, agents who know something do not know everything that is classically equivalent to it. In any situation, they know only finitely many things.

5.3 Views from the Bottom: When Beliefs go Wrong

To understand why we find minimal significance in the distinction between, e.g., Lewis's and Barwise's, accounts of common knowledge requires a look at the ways a mutual understanding can go wrong from a bottom-up perspective. There are at least three ways in which mutual understanding might fail to be veridically grounded. First, it is possible that the base object of that understanding—the proposition about which the mutual belief is held—is itself false. Second, this proposition could be true, but belief in it be based on a jointly held misapprehension. Third, it might be that the base belief is true but based on different misapprehensions.

The first two possibilities are easy to grasp. For example, suppose Eleri and James are running around their house playing. They have a dog, Maggie, and we assume that they have mutually observed Maggie recently playing in a room next to an open door. If they are still together and hear their mother shout that their dog is outside and should be brought in, they naturally form the belief that their dog is outside. Let us further suppose that they do not respond right away, and their father chides them, "Did you hear your mother say that the dog needs to be let in?" If they together answer, "Yes", then conditions are right for them to form not just belief but mutual belief. However, it is possible that their mother was mistaken about their dog being out (perhaps she heard a neighbor's dog outside), or that Maggie came in of her own accord immediately after the shout. In this case the base belief is just false.

For the second possibility, note that Eleri and James also have another dog Danny. Suppose that in addition to the above circumstances they have together recently seen Danny asleep far from any house exit. But suppose, unbeknownst to them, Maggie has just gone into another remote room, while Danny has awakened and quickly gone out—and Danny was the reason for their mother's shout. Now, the base belief 'Our dog is outside.' is true. And, the conditions are adequate for Eleri and James to form a mutual belief in this. But the belief is based on the misapprehension that it is Maggie rather than Danny who is outside.

The third possibility is a little trickier. Recall the card game between James and Eleri. Suppose each of them has an ace in hand. And, suppose James saw Eleri glance at his hand, and Eleri saw James see her glance. This was mutual and direct, no seeing the other in the mirror when s/he perhaps didn't see you or some such. However, James believes Eleri saw his ace when in fact she did not. A moment later the reverse happened: James glanced at Eleri's hand with similar outcome. And, Jennifer, observing these not-so-covert glances, asks them rhetorically, "So, do you know if at least one of you has an ace?" Without any answers, the situation is adequate for them to now have the mutual belief that at least one of them has an ace. However, James believes that they each believe he has an ace and that this is the basis for each of them to believe that at least one of them has an ace and the base of their mutual belief in that. But, Eleri believes that they each believe she has an ace and that this is the basis for each of them to believe that at least one of them has an ace and the base of their mutual belief in that. We see thus that it is possible to have a mutual belief that, if traced to its ultimate roots, is ultimately based on no one fact that is believed by all parties. The mutual belief starts at least one step up from the roots.

Of course this by itself does not limit us to mutual belief rather than common knowledge. Suppose James and Eleri are truthful, and this is common knowledge between them. In the situation we have been discussing, each might utter, "I know that at least one of us has an ace." Given that Eleri already believes there is a common belief that James has seen the ace in her hand and James believes correspondingly about her, they would not expect this to be revealing anything. They can thus have common knowledge that at least one of them has an ace, even though they do not have common knowledge about which of them has an ace.

Notice that for the first two possibilities there is a problem with the basis proposition: it is false or bears the wrong relation to the situation in some Gettier-like[15] fashion, etc. The first of these is an example of mutual belief that is definitely not common knowledge if common knowledge cannot apply to explicitly false propositions. It would thus seem to corroborate that Lewis's definition is too broad. James and Eleri do have reason to believe that they are in a situation where they mutually perceive Maggie to have easy opportunity to go out and their (typically reliable) mother to have said that their dog is outside. And, they are in fact in such a situation. This situation indicates to both of them that both of them have reason to believe they are in this situation. And, this situation indicates to them that their dog (Maggie) is outside. But, it's not actually true that their dog is outside. The second possibility, as illustrated by the case where Danny is outside rather than Maggie, would seem to stand or fall as a case of common knowledge precisely depending on one's view of basic Gettier-style problems. The third possibility may as well, but in a more subtle way that we will discuss below.

5.4 Beliefs in Situations of Coordination

What about cases involving coordination rather than mutual understanding of some arbitrary fact? In coordination as we have described it above, if there is mutual understanding that the parties ought to act in some (coordinated) way, then they do so. The issue is thus only a question of their attaining a mutual understanding that they ought to do some particular thing. If this is a previously mutually understood general principle, then mutual understanding that they ought to coordinate in a particular way implies that they will (try to) coordinate in that particular way. (Call the principle BIMBTOID: belief in mutual belief that ought, implies do.) So, for the two generals, mutual belief that they ought to attack at dawn implies mutual belief that they will both attack at dawn. (We will assume that one cannot try to attack and fail to attack: one can only fail to be victorious in an attack. In other words, we assume that trying to attack is the same as attacking.)

Perhaps this is why Lewis expresses common knowledge in terms of

---

[15]Synopsis of the Gettier problem in too tight a nutshell: Suppose I see something that is reasonable justification of a belief. And the belief is true, but just coincidentally. What I thought I saw was not actually as I perceived it. Is my apparently justified, true belief knowledge in this case? See Moser 1986 for more on the basic problem and responses to it, including a reprint of Gettier 1963.

belief. Simple cases with false but reasonable basis beliefs seem to go against his definition as one of 'common knowledge' in an intuitively reasonable sense. But, Lewis is focused on cases of coordination and convention. And, in these cases, it seems that mutual belief is indeed sufficient for common knowledge. If the two generals ever mutually believe that they will both attack at dawn, then they will each attack at dawn. Not only do they have justified true belief in this case, but given their acceptance of the BIMBTOID principle, the justification is simply that they do have such mutual belief. The justification and truth cannot fail to connect up in the basic Gettier way.

We explore this line further by returning to the third possibility, in which Eleri and James seem to attain mutual belief that at least one of them has an ace, but with a confusion about who has seen what. Here there does seem to be a potential for a disconnect between why it is true and why it is justified. In the third possibility it is the mutuality that is somehow undermined. If we start with the base beliefs of, e.g., James, we see that he can falsely believe that he and Eleri have a mutual belief that he has an ace. It is only about the more subsuming fact that at least one of them has an ace that they can actually have a mutual belief.

How they come to hold this mutual belief may matter. Suppose that James builds his belief in their mutual belief as we described above. More precisely, suppose James believes that he and Eleri mutually believe that he has an ace. And, James believes that if he and Eleri mutually believe that he has an ace, then they will mutually believe that at least one of them has an ace. From these two beliefs he forms the belief that they do mutually believe that at least one of them has an ace. This is a belief about which he could be mistaken. Similarly for Eleri. It would seem that James and Eleri can each believe that they mutually believe that at least one of them has an ace and the justification for this would seem to be distinct from the reason it is true.

This appears to land us back in Gettier territory. And, intent to coordinate by itself is no escape. If Eleri and James mutually decided that mutual belief that one of them has an ace means they ought to act in some coordinated way (e.g., meet at some location tomorrow at noon), then each would on this basis now believe that they had a mutual belief that they ought to do this coordinated act. And, if they held to the BIMBTOID principle, then they would try to do it. To further emphasize the point: If James were questioned out of sight or sound from Eleri, he would be willing to assert that he believes she believes he believes ... that at least one of them has an ace. And, he would ultimately be willing to assert their mutual belief that they will try to meet tomorrow at noon. So, maybe it doesn't matter. Under these circumstances they will meet at noon the next day. Like the generals, they seem to coordinate in spite of themselves. But, if James were to learn that Eleri never saw the ace in his hand, then the entire edifice of their mutual belief would collapse, and with it their coordination. Is the same true for the generals?

To more closely relate the two examples, consider the following variant on the coordinated attack: Suppose the two generals need some secret plans to successfully carry out their attack. These are to be sent from someone else in a remote location via messenger. It does not matter which of them has the plans as long as one of them does. Once one of them has the plans, he sends a message saying "One of us has the plans (so we should attack at dawn)." They then send back and forth similar messages to each other to confirm and build coordination as before. They are also concerned that the enemy not know whether or not they have the secret plans. So, they send messages encrypted under a predistributed cryptographic key that they share with each other (and no one else). To better hide from the enemy when and if one of them receives the plans, they exchange encrypted "Don't got it yet." messages at regular intervals.[16] To make sure they can distinguish messages that they themselves have sent as well as ones they have received previously, each encrypted message contains an indicator based on a fairly standard cryptographic trick called a reverse hash chain.

Put very briefly, a hash function, h, is one that takes arbitrary input, i, and produces a fixed-size output, $o = h(i)$, such that, given i it is easy to confirm or compute that $o = h(i)$. But, given just o (and h), it is computationally infeasible to find i. See Menezes et al. 1997 for more details. A reverse hash chain is formed by repeatedly hashing a random value some large number of times n. The first element of the chain is then the nth hash of the random value. As each link up the chain is revealed, it is easy to confirm that it is the next link up by confirming that its hash is the most recent previously revealed link. Given any revealed link, it is easy to confirm that the later revealed links are values in the chain and to confirm how much farther down the chain they are. But, it is infeasible to predict any value up the chain before it has been revealed.

The generals each build a reverse hash chain based on a good (pseudo)random seed and long enough to far exceed the number of

---

[16]For the cryptographically savvy reader, assume that all messages contain a random salt. More generally, I make no claims for the general security quality of this protocol. That's not my purpose.

messages that might be sent. A new link from the sending general's reverse hash chain is included inside each encrypted message sent. Receiving a message that is more than one up the chain from the previous received message is OK: To provide some robustness against loss of a single message, generals will send up to some number, e.g., three times, while awaiting the last expected response. Each sent message contains a new link in the hash chain. Each of the generals keeps track of the links he has sent and those he has received.

Suppose that both generals receive the secret plans at the same time. They then will both begin sending announcements that one of them has the plans. Suppose further that the initially sent messages do not arrive, at least not in a timely fashion. So each general has sent, e.g., two or three messages saying that one of them has the plans. Especially if they had not considered the possibility that both would receive the plans (and even more especially at the same time), then general A will understand the first message from B that they should attack at dawn as a response to A's notice that he has the plans rather than as an indication that B has the plans. B will be under the same misapprehension about A.

The generals are now in a situation roughly analogous to that of James and Eleri. Assume for the moment that the actions of the generals yield common knowledge—or at least mutual belief. (We will return to argue this in the next section.) Then, general A believes that they have mutual belief that he has the plans, and general B believes that they have mutual belief that he has the plans. And, it seems that based on this, they have mutual beliefs that (1) at least one of them has the plans, (2) they ought to attack at dawn, and (3) they will attack at dawn.

How tight is the analogy between the two situations? Recall that if James found out that Eleri had not seen his ace, it undid his beliefs and with them his expectation that they will meet tomorrow at noon. What if general A found out somehow that general B did not think that A had the secret plans? If A assumes B to be basically rational, he cannot just abandon his previous beliefs, because unlike James, he has received several distinct messages indicating that B believes one of them has the secret plans and thinks they should attack at dawn. Unless A actually considers at that point that B might have his own copy of the plans, he will have to conclude that B is irrational or deceptive, or that some other oddness has occurred. Similarly, if James had independent reason for thinking that Eleri believed that at least one of them had an ace, for example, if he had overheard her say so, then the reasonable conclusion for him to make would be that she must have one. The beliefs of the generals interconnect in a way that those of James and Eleri do not. One action, a single physical occasion that James and Eleri share is the basis for all subsequent beliefs. But, the generals have multiple actions for which to account.

These are not causally independent; the generals send messages in a chain of ping pong exchanges (with at most a few extra messages possible at each exchange). But, these are empirically distinct actions and events. And, though the generals are expected to follow the exchange protocol, other than this the physical actions involved in the sending of each message are relatively independent, and each sending implies an independent decision to continue the exchange. One can construct elaborate philosophical examples in which ever more layers of belief (knowledge) about each other's beliefs are piled on some proposition by new actions and observations, while still maintaining reasons for questioning the next layer (Clark and Marshall 1981). But, at some point these become cognitively untenable; one cannot keep track of distinct events. That the layers have gotten higher based on distinct actions can only be recognized by conceptually gathering up the actions, for example, recognizing that more stuff of the kind already observed has happened. As, we will discuss in section 6.2, this is what is needed to provide the level of mutuality in common knowledge (or mutual understanding in general). But, our purpose here is to examine the ways in which mutual understanding fails. In particular, we are now examining ways a belief in mutual belief could fail. (This would be a failure of what Bonanno and Nehring (2000) call *intersubjective caution* because people are willing to believe in a mutual belief without knowing that it is a mutual belief.) To undermine or undo the mutual understanding in this case would require some systematic reinterpretation of the actions that gave rise to that belief in mutual understanding. We now look at some of the ways this could occur.

Knowing Who You're Talking to

Suppose James observes on several distinct occasions someone asking Eleri, "Do you believe that he believes that... at least one of you has an ace?" Suppose that there generally seem to be more layers of belief in later questions than earlier and that on each occasion James hears Eleri assent to the question. He seems to be in a situation more tightly analogous to the generals. Suppose he then observes her being asked if she has seen any aces in James's hand and observes her saying "no". He might conclude that she must have her own ace. However, he might also conclude that she had not been talking about him when she assented to all those beliefs about "at least one of you has an ace". So, it is possible to undo the connections associated with all of those distinct events in a single observation.

Such a systematic cancellation of all the beliefs held by the generals is also possible. It could be that each is communicating with some other party. For example, the enemy could be sending responses to general A but not general B in the hope of causing one of the generals to attack alone. More specifically, this could be an expansion on the original scenario. It could not happen in the more elaborate circumstances involving encryption that we set out above as long as the key used to encrypt the messages and shared between the generals remains secret to the two of them, and as long as they can differentiate and keep track of previously sent messages (and they each faithfully follow the expected exchange and no other).

There are various complexities that arise when you don't know who you're talking to, or sometimes even when you do. The interested reader is invited to construct scenarios in which James is in fact talking to Eleri and believes he is talking to Eleri, but he is carrying on multiple conversations with her and is confused as to which things were said by each of them and which are part of which conversation. This can be of genuine concern and it is possible to construct attacks on authenticated key distribution protocols when such confusions occur (Syverson and Cervesato 2001). Alternatively, James can think he is talking just to Eleri when he is actually talking to both Eleri and Melissa, and he might believe he shares a mutual belief with *the* person he is talking to, when in fact there is no single other holder of that belief. However, in cases of conventional behavior, except perhaps those with an adversary actively trying to create and exploit confusion, such scenarios are conceptually possible but very unlikely. This is because, as noted, there are multiple occasions when evidence is given (1) of what is understood, (2) that the understanding is mutual, and (3) of who is mutually understanding. In the situation where James hears Eleri deny knowing that he has an ace after all of the glancing and corroborations that she knows that at least one of "them" has an ace, it is easy to see revising of (1) what is understood and why. Given some appropriate ancillary information, one could imagine James revising his idea of (3) who it is that formed a mutual understanding. But note that James would have a hard time making sense of the idea that Eleri does not believe she has a mutual understanding with someone that at least one of them has an ace. Of course she might be mistaken in that belief (another violation of intersubjective caution). But it is hard to do away with mutual understanding outright. Thus, in cases where there is confusion about who is mutually understanding a convention, there is still a mutual understanding. In conventional behavior, if such confusion is cleared up or at least exposed, this may kill the convention in the sense that (some of) those involved will choose not to continue. But, there was still a convention, even if those who convened now wish otherwise. Indeed, even in cases where some agent has mistaken the actions of multiple others in a systematic way to constitute a convention, he would still have engaged in convention. It would just be different conventions than he thought and with different individuals than he thought. But, in another way he would still have engaged in a convention, even the one he thought, just with an agent who was not the person he thought it was. We will return to such points in chapter 10.

5.5 Belief-based Common Knowledge in Conventions

So far we have noted that Lewis's definition of common knowledge was actually one of mutual (or common) belief. And, we have observed ways in which mutually held beliefs could be incorrect, or at least problematic. We noted that, assuming the attacking generals actually obtain mutual belief, their mutual belief is supported in ways that mutual beliefs were not in most of our other examples. Specifically, they received multiple distinct indications that the belief is mutually held. To undo this mutual belief would require a systematic reinterpretation of the significance of all observed events. Even if that were the case there would still appear to have been at least some mutual understanding of something by someone. In the case of the generals, what has been mutually agreed is relatively clear, and, if we add the further assumptions about protecting and authenticating the communication, then it is also clear who has agreed.

All of this means that the mutual belief of the generals cannot be problematic in the manner of our other examples. This is not quite enough, however, because it is just mutual belief. But, we saw that mutual belief in an intent to coordinate in a specific way implies that intent. Thus, this mutual belief cannot go astray, absent a systematic reinterpretation that we have already ruled out.

Cases of coordination that are conventional are ones in which there is a regularity in the behavior of those convening to which almost everyone conforms. We noted in section 3.2 that there may be problems deciding what constitutes a regularity. And, it is certainly possible that one person's perceived regularity is different from another's. This could be because of a difference of perception on who is convening—as we have just described—or because there just happens to be enough overlap in the distinct regularities themselves that coordination has so far been achieved.

The more that coordination is reinforced, however, the more it would be hard to argue that there are multiple regularities that simply coincided rather than some larger regularity of which the distinct perceived regularities are a part. And, if the coordination later fell apart, we would be inclined to say that the convention had changed or that the actions were no longer conventional rather than that they had never been so at all. Lewis takes from Hume the example of two people rowing a boat smoothly and in a straight line, each with one oar. The physical aspects of the coordinated action may be hard to capture verbally. But, Lewis's account assumes that they would agree with his characterization of their behavior as conventional, up to the limits of their rational abilities. Our point here is that, if they should after some large number of strokes fall out of synch, we would still want to say their behavior was conventional until that point.

Convention arises in circumstances with enough evidential reinforcement to overcome any ordinary level of skepticism, and in which the mutually held belief is about intention to act on the part of those mutually holding that belief. These are the kinds of mutual belief that were the focus of Lewis (1969). And, for the reasons we have been discussing, such mutual beliefs do constitute common knowledge.

6
The Origins of Mutual Understanding

Amongst other things, in the previous chapter we went to some length to show that if the two generals have a mutual belief that they will attack, then they actually have common knowledge that they will attack. But we still have not explained how they come to have any such mutual understanding in the first place. This chapter is focused on the question of how people can come to have mutual understanding of anything at all.

6.1 Intrinsic Vagueness

We first note a similarity between the inductive argument given by Halpern & Moses concerning the failure of the generals to obtain common knowledge (quoted above in section 4.3) and the *sorites* paradox or, as it is also known, the fallacy of the heap. Stated briefly it says: One grain of sand is clearly not a heap. Assume for induction that n grains of sand is insufficient to make a heap. Clearly adding one grain of sand to n others, which do not constitute a heap, will not be sufficient to make a heap. Thus, for any n, n grains of sand is insufficient to constitute a heap. We know this argument does not work because it proves that there are no heaps of sand, which is empirically false. At least one explanation of what is wrong with this argument is that 'heap' denotes a vague concept. There are no sharp boundaries to what constitutes a heap, but the inductive argument presupposes that there are.[17] Perhaps the same could be said about the concept of common knowledge or at least common knowledge in the described circumstances. As long as we keep the criteria for common knowledge vague we can attain it; if we try to stipulate precise requirements we cannot. I think this is

---

[17]For a more detailed discussion of these issues cf. Black 1970b.

ultimately true; however, there is an important disanalogy between the common knowledge argument and the heap.

In the case of the heap we can simply stipulate some number n as that number of grains of sand necessary for a heap. This may not reflect actual usage, but, as with most vague concepts, such a move leaves us with a meaningful concept that we can still apply. This is not the case for common knowledge of a coordinated attack attained in the manner described in section 4.4. Here the concept seems to be intrinsically vague: if we try to make it precise, it is no longer applicable. For, no matter what number n of messages we set, we will be able to apply the inductive argument of Halpern & Moses. The heap argument is defeated when we stipulate a boundary because the inductive step no longer holds. There is a number n such that n grains do not constitute a heap, but $n+1$ grains do. But, in the coordinated attack, if n messages to each general suffice for common knowledge, after n messages at least one of the generals will not know that they have attained common knowledge. This result seems to undercut the usefulness of precisely demarcated common knowledge in a way that does not arise for precisely demarcated heaps.

This is more than a merely practical point. For, if n messages to each general were to suffice, then they actually would have common knowledge here—assuming the last general receives the nth message. But, they would lack common knowledge of their common knowledge and would be unable to use their common knowledge in any standard way, such as providing justification for attacking at dawn. This point thus serves to finally illustrate why it is necessary that common knowledge of φ imply common knowledge of common knowledge of φ. Not only is this requirement reasonable, but in its absence our notion of common knowledge becomes overtly counterintuitive.

Even though the above disanalogy exists between common knowledge in a distributed situation and other types of vague concepts, it only says something about the possibility of making the concept precise. It does not indicate a problem for attaining common knowledge in distributed situations as long as things are kept vague in the right way. But even if we cannot give a precise number of messages that constitute common knowledge in the coordinated attack case, we can still be precise in our characterization of it.

Before we leave the topic of vagueness it is important to note how vagueness indicates a limitation of our solution to the coordinated attack problem. It is a solution to the problem as presented by Halpern & Moses, but it may fail for similar cases. The very nature of vague concepts is such that there is a hazy range of cases where we are unsure whether the concept applies or not. Suppose the generals agree that an adequate number of messages is roughly several more than n. Suppose then that A receives $n+4$ messages and no more. B has thus received either $n+3$ or $n+4$ messages. Is this sufficient for common knowledge? Should A attack? We are in that hazy area, and it is just unclear what to say. In their characterization of the problem, Halpern & Moses stipulate that on this particular night all messages get through more or less on time. Thus the generals can be sure that they have a whole heap of common knowledge. In other situations they may not be so sure. Of course in such situations they should not attack. If a general isn't sure whether he has common knowledge, then presumably he doesn't believe that he has common knowledge. Under the constraints of the problem this means he shouldn't attack. Attack is not prescribed along the fuzzy border of common knowledge but only in the clear-cut cases. The unavoidable danger is that, when both of them have received as much information as they are going to, one general might feel he has moved from the fuzzy border to a clear case while the other one does not. To *this* problem there is no solution. Nonetheless, what we have seen is that, contrary to popular belief, clear cases of common knowledge do exist even in distributed situations.

Defeasibility and Co-Induction

In order to give a more precise characterization of common knowledge in the coordinated attack case it will be useful to contrast it with a clearer case of common knowledge. Perhaps the quintessential case of common knowledge is that involving copresence. If our generals were face to face, there would be no question about their ability to coordinate an attack. This is not simply because communication is guaranteed but because of their epistemic relation to this fact. It might seem that the difference is just that in the one case they know that communication is guaranteed but in the other they can doubt the success of any attempt at communication. In other words, in the distributed case their knowledge is defeasible but in the copresent case it is not. This, however, is too simple. Knowledge is defeasible in both situations. Even face to face, either general can doubt whether or not the other heard him, whether the other understood him, whether he understood the other, etc. But, there is a difference in the defeasibility. We can explore this difference by looking at inductive arguments for the two cases, and we will do so presently.

As we have already seen, even clear cases of common knowledge seem paradoxical in that they seem to require an infinite number of inferences in a finite amount of time. Perhaps there is no genuine paradox here. As Lewis (1969) points out, "this is a chain of implications, not of steps in anyone's actual reasoning. Therefore there is nothing improper about its infinite length" (p. 53). We will return to situations sufficient to guarantee common knowledge presently; however, even if we can easily characterize situations that we can finitely recognize and that are sufficient for common knowledge, we still must give an account of our ability to finitely recognize that sufficiency—i.e. to finitely recognize the situation as a situation of common knowledge. We can illustrate this by means of an inductive argument concerning the two generals, this time a positive one.

To simplify matters we consider only how the generals attain common knowledge that A said "We should attack at dawn." (We symbolize this using 'p'.) This can simply be repeated to explain how they attain common knowledge that B said "I agree." I now give an inductive argument that, for any n, a chain of iterated knowledge attributions of length n is justified in the situation of copresence we have described. The base case is trivial: A obviously knows that he said "We should attack at dawn." Assume for inductive hypothesis that we have a chain, A knows B knows ... A knows p. with n iterations. How can B justify that he knows this? He is justified in making this inductive inference because he has no reason to differentiate it from the last several similar inferences that (by hypothesis) he has already accepted. Put another way, at some point general B loses the ability to differentiate a heap of knowledge from a heap with two more grains in it (or two less). And, B knows this. Thus, B knows that if A is justified in believing that B knows A knows ... A knows p, then B is justified in believing that A knows that. Because it is indistinguishable from the case with two less knowledge attributions in it. And, by hypothesis, he was already justified in believing that. So, he is justified in making the inductive inference because in this situation he has every reason to accept it and no reason to doubt it. That justification actually makes this something of a co-inductive argument rather than a straightforward inductive one. In other words, he only rejects inferences that he has some reason to reject. Absent that, he accepts the inference. As was already noted, Barwise (1989a) uses such a co-inductive argument for his definition of the satisfaction relation. This co-inductive justification of the inductive step is how the generals can finitely justify to themselves any of the entries in the entirety of the infinite iterated hierarchy. Put colloquially, the justification is "Why not?"

How does this compare with the distributed situation? Here it seems that the general cannot make the inductive inference so easily. For, the situation is constrained so that, given a chain of iterated knowledge attributions of length n, we have a specific reason for doubting the $n+1^{st}$ attribution, viz the $n+1^{st}$ message may have been lost because the courier was lost or delayed in the woods or even captured. How then were we able to solve the problem above? In effect we allowed the co-inductive move to go through by preempting the doubt of the inductive inference. Indeed, in the last chapter we saw that it was easier to undermine mutual understanding in situations like that of the copresent generals than in the distributed case because there is not the same level of independent evidence for common knowledge.

So, given the situation they were in, the generals had enough evidence to justify all the possibilities they were willing to consider. As Halpern and Moses (1990) point out, "the actions that should be taken depend not only on the actual state of affairs (in this case, the messenger successfully delivering the messages), but also (in an acute way) on what other states of affairs the generals consider *possible*" (p. 557). In our solution they agreed to refuse to consider the possibilities where doubt could be introduced. This will be explained in more detail below.

6.2 The Vague Shared-Situation Approach

We have given a solution to the coordinated attack problem, but we have not explicitly shown how this yields common knowledge. As an example, we give a particular shared situation sufficient for the two generals to attain common knowledge. Let s be a situation in which the following are true: A and B have agreed previously that several more than, e.g., five messages sent to each of them will be sufficient for common knowledge that p, where 'p' denotes that they both want the attack to be at the time specified in the first message. They have each actually received several more than five messages. (Let's assume that they have actually received exactly twelve messages each, though neither one has this exact figure. This fact is *not* part of the situation s.) They each know that they have each received several more than five messages. Then,

- $s \models p$
- $s \models A$ knows s.
- $s \models B$ knows s.

In other words, s is a shared situation sufficient for A and B to have common knowledge that p.

While the shared-situation approach does provide a basis for common knowledge, its structure does not incorporate the vagueness that we found to be inherent in common knowledge. This vagueness can be represented in specific situations that satisfy the requirements of the approach. In this sense it is a clear advance over the iterated approach in which such vagueness cannot be represented. However, since situations that are not vague can also satisfy the requirements of the approach, the approach per se does not represent the vague nature of common knowledge. It thus seems to lack the cognitive element that one would expect in common *knowledge*. However, this just shows a flexibility in the approach. Whether or not the cognitive element is captured is reflected by the type of situation in which the common knowledge arises.

Shared Information vs. Common Knowledge

In order to see the significance of the type of situation in which common knowledge arises it is helpful to have a distinction that Barwise makes between informational and epistemic readings of 'common knowledge'. On the informational reading someone has common knowledge just in case they have all the information logically contained in the situation of common knowledge. Thus, it is actually meaningful to distinguish 'A knows B knows A knows B knows A knows B knows A knows B knows A knows B knows A knows B knows p.' from 'A knows B knows A knows B knows A knows B knows A knows B knows p.'On the epistemic reading, it is at least unclear that we can make such a distinction. There is a cognitive element in the notion. It is not that we can't represent the distinction between these two statements in a meaningful way: one has ten occurrences of 'knows', the other twelve. But, we cannot easily comprehend the difference between the actual attributions. At some point, the distinction ceases to be meaningful for us. This is what is captured by an account involving vague situations and what makes it a better account of common *knowledge*.

Fagin et al. (1995) espouse an informational reading while considering the cognitive element when they show that there is a value k such that if everyone has k layers of knowledge about everyone's knowledge of φ, then they have common knowledge that φ. As they explain on p. 388, the reason this is compatible with the impossibility proof for the coordinated attack is that the k must always be larger than at least some agent's ability to differentiate states, much in the way we have just been considering. As they put it, one of our generals always cannot count high enough. What Fagin et al. do not discuss is the ability of agents to ignore distinctions in the way we are exploring here. This is a basic aspect of the epistemic view.

We noted above that, in a situation of copresence, coordination is possible not simply because communication is guaranteed but because of the epistemic relation the generals bear to this fact. The vague account more accurately represents this epistemic relation than does the standard shared-situation account. For, the vague account gives some insight into the bootstrapping justification of the inductive step. (Hereafter we distinguish between shared-situation characterizations of common knowledge by calling those explicitly involving vague situations 'the vague account' or 'the vague approach' and ones not explicitly involving vague situations 'the standard account'.) The first few iterations can actually be justified directly. At some point, however, the general ceases to make a clear distinction between n and $n-2$ iterations, and he is unsure whether he has justified n iterations or not. On the vague account, if s is a situation in which n justifications have been made, then in his current situation he doesn't know whether s is the situation or not. Thus, on the epistemic reading of 'common knowledge', of the accounts we have discussed, the vague account provides the best characterization of both the copresent coordinated attack and the distributed coordinated attack.

The informational reading implicit in the standard account is consistent with a co-inductive definition that permits the inclusion of all of the layers of knowledge we might ever need. Put another way, it shows how we can have a finite situation that is sufficient for common knowledge. But it fails to say how we actually get in such a shared situation in the first place. For this, it is not enough to give a mathematically coherent and precise account of such situations. The intuitive appeal of the iterative approach is surely that it demonstrates how we build to common knowledge. It's failing is in not showing how we can ever quite arrive there. The fixed-point and standard shared-situation approaches account for the view once we arrive, but fail to account for the journey. What is needed is an account that covers both the journey and the destination, that provides both the inductive and co-inductive elements. As Barwise (1989a) says, "What suffices in order for common knowledge to be useful is that it arise in some fairly straightforward shared situation. The reason this is useful is that such shared situations provide a basis for perceivable situated action, action that then produces further shared situations." This is especially so in explaining conventions, and is what the vague account provides.

We are not claiming that the vague account is uniformly better than the standard situational account, or indeed the fixed-point or iterated accounts. In some contexts, the standard situational account is more appropriate than the vague account. For example, in designing protocols for coordination in distributed computing, even when taking into account probabilistic or complexity-theoretic limitations on knowledge, the standard account is more useful.[18] Such limitations may make it seem that we are concerned with the epistemic reading of 'common knowledge' in these contexts; nevertheless it is not necessary to use vague situations because the criteria for being in the situation remain precisely statable, albeit in terms of probabilities or computational complexities.

Barwise 1989a notes of itself that "the best way to understand the work here is not so much in terms of common knowledge, but in terms of shared information. But, I would argue, the same is true of almost all work that purports to be about common knowledge, since it is done under assumptions that are reasonable for information, but unreasonable for knowledge." This chapter and this book in general are a self-conscious attempt to do work that is best understood in terms of common knowledge, rather than shared information. What we have tried to explain in the last few chapters is how people can finitely recognize, especially through growing evidence, that they are in a situation that is indeed one of common knowledge. We showed that there were situations sufficient for common knowledge that were indeed sufficient for mutual expectation to commit a coordinated action. And, we showed how such situations could arise and what their structure would be. In so doing, we left several technical semantic notions unexplained. These are set out in the next three chapters.

---

[18] For a discussion of probabilistic common knowledge and coordination cf. Tuttle 1990, chap. 4. For a discussion of common knowledge and coordination under complexity theoretic constraints cf. Moses 1988. Or for both of these cf. Fagin et al. 1995.

7
A Logic of Familiarity

The logical representation of knowledge has to date been primarily focussed on propositional knowledge, knowledge *that*. But, there is another use of 'know' in English that has received little attention in developed formal systems. This is the knowledge of an individual in the sense of familiarity. We are speaking here of statements of the form of 'Eleri knows Nancy.' [19] The well known *de re/de dicto* distinction has helped us to explore, for example, the difference between knowing that Nancy is Eleri's aunt and knowing of Nancy that she is Eleri's aunt. This gives us a sort of direct representation of knowledge of individuals, but it does not give us the ability to represent knowing Nancy *simpliciter*, i.e., without mention of any particular facts about her. Hintikka (1962) does present a rather extensive discussion of "knowing who". We will discuss the essential differences between his approach and ours below in section 8.1.

'Familiarity' generally carries a connotation of close acquaintance, far more so in fact than ordinary concepts of knowledge. The precise meaning of our expressions will be given below when we set out our semantics. However, we offer a brief intuitive discussion now. In our logic of familiarity, if Eleri is familiar with Nancy, then she has a full acquaintance with everything about about her. Thus, Eleri either knows Nancy or she doesn't. In every circumstance in which Eleri knows Nancy, she knows whatever is true of Nancy in that circumstance. And, if Eleri knows anything about Nancy, then she is completely familiar with her. More discussion of this notion of familiarity and its expressive limitations are discussed below and in the next chapter.

One of our ultimate goals is to provide a logic for formally representing the shared situation account of common knowledge, as discussed in

---

[19]Some of the content of this chapter previously appeared in somewhat different form in Syverson 1990.

previous chapters. This is broken into roughly two parts. The logic set out in this chapter is meant to lay part of the groundwork by introducing the representation of familiarity. This is interesting in its own right; however, it is not sufficient for this ultimate goal. To accomplish this, other features are added in the logic of awareness given in chapter 9. The developments of chapter 9 will obviate some of the technical aspects of the present chapter. Nonetheless, in getting where we need to go, I have found it conceptually useful to set out the progression of ideas in this way, rather than skipping straight to the end.

7.1 The Language

The language contains a denumerable supply of individual constant symbols: a, b, c, ... These serve as names for individuals and may or may not have subscripts. We also have individual variables: x, y, z, ..., also with or without subscripts. These are the atomic terms. They can be combined via function symbols to build up compound terms in the usual recursive manner. Our language also contains denumerably many predicate constants: P, Q, R, ..., each of finite arity and taking tuples of individual constants as arguments. We generally do not indicate the arity of predicate constants. If necessary this is done via superscripts. Predicate symbols also may or may not be subscripted. Of the predicate constants, we call particular attention to a set of unary epistemic predicate constants: C_1, C_2, ..., C_n. We will also write these with individual names as subscripts. Intuitively, $C_b(a)$ should be taken to mean that b knows a, i.e., b can recognize a. This will be explained in detail below. We also have the identity symbol, $=$.

The language is first order. The basic (open) sentences of the language are expressions of the form $P(x_1, \ldots, x_j)$ or $P(a_1, \ldots, a_j)$. Closed sentences are those containing no free variables. Sentences (open or closed) may be assembled into (finite) complex sentences according to ordinary recursive formation rules using the usual connectives: $\neg$, $\wedge$, $\vee$, $\rightarrow$, and $\leftrightarrow$ with the usual scope assumptions and using the usual delimiters (parentheses and brackets). The only remaining basic feature of the language is a finite set of propositional knowledge operators: S_1, S_2, ..., S_n. These are standard epistemic operators in the tradition of Hintikka (1962). Intuitively $S_a\varphi$ should be taken to mean that a knows the proposition expressed by φ.[20] (φ is a metalinguistic variable rang-

---

[20]The choice of symbols for knowledge derives from the French words '*connâitre*' and '*savoir*'. For example, in French, you *connais* a person but you *sais* that it's raining. English does not distinguish these senses and translates both words as 'to know'. (Actually, especially in Scottish dialectical English, the word 'ken' is used essentially like *connâitre*. Unfortunately, this does not help us make the notational

ing over arbitrary sentences.) $S_a\varphi$ is a sentence, provided that φ is a sentence. Thus these operators may be iterated.

7.2 Semantics

Basic Concepts

The semantics we adopt is an offshoot of the standard Hintikka style possible world semantics for epistemic logics.[21] Unlike the standard semantics, however, our possible worlds will be partial. Thus, the semantics is also rooted in the tradition of Barwise and Perry's situation semantics (Barwise and Perry 1983, Barwise 1989b). This background information is given merely to provide context, and the influence of the above cited works on the present work is essentially motivational. The logic and semantics presented herein also owes some of its motivation to free logic (Bencivenga 1986) and to the work of Garson (1984).

Before we begin to set things out formally we give an intuitive picture of some of the basic concepts. First there is a set of possible worlds. These can be thought of as different ways the world may be conceived to be. On this set there are accessibility relations, one for each individual. If world w' is accessible from world w for a given individual, then that individual at w cannot distinguish the two worlds (given his current state of knowledge). So, suppose there are two worlds that are accessible to each other for individual a. In one of these worlds it is currently raining where a is, and in the other it is not. In this case, a does not know whether or not it's raining (relative to either world). If a sentence φ is true in all worlds accessible for a from a given world w, then we say that a knows φ in w.

Most epistemic logics in the distributed computing and economics literatures are or contain the system **S5**. Thus, since the accessibility relations are equivalences, they are often referred to as "indiscernibility" relations. That is, each one partitions the set of worlds into subsets that are equivalent, i.e., indiscernible, for the relevant individual. We will see below that, as in Hintikka 1962, our accessibility relation is not symmetric. Therefore, we will continue to use the more general terminology. In the philosophical literature, epistemic logics generally do not contain **S5**. For example, Hintikka (1962) explicitly rules out negative introspection, the **5** axiom (*op. cit.*, p. 106). (Hintikka has more epistemic modalities available, e.g., for all that a knows. This allows him

---

distinction we need.)

[21]Except where discussing the generally recognized differences, such as in this paragraph, we use the expressions 'world', 'possible world', and 'situation' interchangeably in this chapter.

76 / Logic, Convention, and Common Knowledge

to propose the more reasonable introspective conditions: $(C. \sim K)$ If a does not know φ, then for all that a knows $\neg \varphi$. and $(C. \sim P)$ If for all that a knows $\neg \varphi$, then a does not know φ.)

The above corresponds to our characterization of propositional knowledge by means of the S operators. For knowledge characterized by the C predicates, we maintain the same semantic structure of worlds and accessibility relations; we simply add to it. In quantified modal logic one decides whether, for example $P(x_1, \ldots, x_k)$ is true at a world by seeing if the k-tuple of values assigned to x_1 through x_k respectively at that world is in the set assigned to P at that world. The same criterion applies to sentences formed with the C predicates, but with a somewhat unusual twist. Except for identity, predicates usually get their interpretation extralogically. The interpretation of the C predicates is intimately tied to the semantic structure itself. $C_a x$ is true at world w_n whenever x is assigned a value at w_n and it is assigned the same value at all worlds accessible from w_n for a. Since these predicates are rather unusual, we will give a little explanation of their semantic interpretation.

In order to further understand the C predicates it is necessary to grasp a fundamental difference in the way possible worlds are to be thought of in our semantics. Ordinarily, possible worlds are construed as different ways the world might be. These are metaphysical possibilities and the modality that they naturally engender is alethic. Nonetheless, these same possible worlds are ordinarily used to underly epistemic logic. Knowledge is represented as the ability to discriminate amongst all the ontologically given possible worlds. But, if our logic is to be one of epistemic rather than alethic modality, then this should be reflected in the worlds that engender that modality. Thus, our worlds are construed as different ways the world might be conceived. Pursuing this intuitive explanation any further without any technical development is likely to make it a counterintuitive explanation. However, I hope that it gives us enough background to make intuitive sense of the C predicates.

If a world w' is accessible from world w for Addie, then at world w, she cannot tell them apart. From the perspective of world w, Addie finds both w and w' equally possible ways things might be. Now, suppose some individual, Bob, is present at one of these worlds but not at the other. (What 'present' means will be clearer once the model theory is spelled out below.) Then Addie cannot tell the difference between a world where Bob is present and one where he is not. So, she must not really be aware of Bob, *know* Bob, if she can't tell whether he's there or not. Under these circumstances we would not want to say that she can recognize, that she knows, Bob. Thus, if 'C_a' picks out who

Addie knows in our language and 'b' names Bob in our language, then it should turn out that $C_a(b)$ is not true at w.

We look at one more example to further bring out the implications of having epistemic worlds. Consider a situation in which baby Jenna knows Aunt Nancy. In this situation Aunt Nancy can know that Jenna knows her but can imagine that Jenna might not know her. This level of understanding is beyond Jenna's capabilities. Indeed, Jenna cannot even introspectively understand what it would mean for her to know that she knows Aunt Nancy. Thus, we have a world w in which Nancy is present. However, for Nancy to accept in w that Jenna might not know her, from w there must be a world w' accessible to both Jenna and Nancy in which Nancy is present and a world w'' accessible only to Jenna from w' at which Nancy is not present. w' is accessible from w, and w'' is accessible from w'. Thus, if accessibility were transitive, w'' would be accessible from w. This would rule out our ability to represent the above scenario. It is a standard result[22] that transitivity in the accessibility relation corresponds to the presence of the **4** axiom (sometimes called positive introspection) in the logic. Thus, even though this axiom has traditionally been accepted for epistemic logic all the way back to Hintikka (1962), we will reject it.

In addition to the aforementioned philosophical reasons for not having a standard possible world semantics we have a technical motivation as well. If every term of the language were to denote in every world, and if terms always denoted the same individual regardless of the world, then all agents would know all individuals in all circumstances—assuming all the individuals are named by the language. This is so because all the worlds would have the same individuals in them, and those individuals would be named the same way at each of them. This would render the C predicates trivial and thus useless. The answer of course is to vary the domain of quantification from world to world. This will block the validity of $\forall x C_i x$ as long as there are things in the domain of quantification of some world that are not in the domain of quantification of another.[23] Unfortunately this strategy is not sufficient to entirely solve the problem. For, even with the domains varying, a constant term will (by definition) denote the same individual in all worlds. Thus any individual that is given a name in our language will be an individual that everyone always knows. Somehow we need to have terms that may not denote at all possible worlds. Fortunately, there is a way

---

[22]Cf., e.g. Chellas 1980.
[23]Note that this also provides a semantic guarantee that the Carnap-Barcan Formula is not valid. We will return to this below where it will be seen to be a desirable result.

to deal directly with nondenoting singular terms.

Bencivenga (1986) defines a free logic as "a formal system of quantification theory, with or without identity, which allows for some singular terms in some circumstances to be thought of as denoting no existing object, and in which quantifiers are invariably thought of as having existential import" (p. 375). This is just what we need to solve the above technical problems, provided that we fill in the details properly. Note that while we adopt some of the machinery of free logic, our goals are very different. The reader should not make any of the usual presumptions about what this approach to quantification accomplishes. In particular, the existential quantifier has more to do with whether or not a term is meaningful or understood than with whether or not it picks out an existing individual. That is, we are not so much using it to tell whether or not Pegasus exists as to tell whether or not 'Pegasus' is understood to mean anything. (Recall the above discussion of what it means for an individual to be in the domain of a given world.)

In effect, our strategy here is to adopt the proposal given by Bencivenga, namely to vary the domain of quantification from world to world. All we need do is incorporate the correct interpretation of terms into this picture. A singular term t denotes at a world just in case it names a member of the domain of quantification at that world, i.e., $\exists x(x = t)$ is true at that world (where x is a variable distinct from t). For ease of expression we define a predicate expressed by 'M' such that $M(t) =_{df} \exists x(x = t)$, where x is a variable distinct from t. In free logic, this definition is a way of getting at what exists; thus, it might seem more natural to use 'E' rather than 'M'. But, we are trying to get at what is understood, known—in the sense of the C-predicates. Therefore, we have chosen 'M' as a mnemonic for terms that are *meaningful* in an epistemic situation.[24] Now, the usual rule for universal instantiation says something like, from $\forall x \varphi$ infer $\varphi[t/x]$. For us the rule is from $\forall x \varphi \wedge Mt$ infer $\varphi[t/x]$. Similarly, we universally generalize on φ only if $Mt \rightarrow \varphi$. Of course this is merely an intuitive description of quantification. The proper explication will come in the following section. But, this should give an idea of why, in our logic, quantification always presumes meaningful terms, just as in free logic it always has existential import.

---

[24]This should in no way be confused with the use of 'M' for a possibility operator as in, e.g., Hughes and Cresswell 1968. (No notation is perfect. Suggestions for a good belnap here would be appreciated.)

Models

A model is a tuple $\langle W, R_1, \ldots R_n, D, d, a \rangle$ where W is a set of nonempty possible worlds; $R_1, \ldots, R_n$ are reflexive (binary) accessibility relations between members of W; and D is a domain of objects for all possible worlds. d is a function from members of W to subsets of D. Thus, $d(w)$ is the domain at world w. (It may seem somewhat contrary to our epistemic view of possible worlds to have a given domain for all the worlds at once. But, this is just a matter of technical convenience. If so desired, we could replace D and d with a set of domains $\{d_w\}_{w \in W}$ given for each world. It is trivial to start from a model of either type and define a model of the other type.) a is an assignment function, which assigns semantic values to expressions in our language in the manner given below. Since we want to allow a to be undefined sometimes, we use the standard trick of adding a value '$*$' to represent being undefined. This allows us to have an assignment function that is total and yet still gives us a means to say that terms sometimes fail to denote and sentences sometimes do not have a definite truth value.[25]

The Assignment Function

The assignment function assigns semantic values to syntactic entities as follows:

$a(t) \in D$ \hfill for all terms t

$a(\langle t_1, \ldots, t_k \rangle) = \langle a(t_1), \ldots, a(t_k) \rangle$ \hfill where $t_1, \ldots, t_k$ are terms

(We suppress tuple notation below when it is clear what is meant.)
$a(f(t_1, \ldots, t_k)) = a(f)(a(t_1, \ldots, t_k)) =$ \hfill where $t_1, \ldots, t_k$ are terms,
$= a(f)(a(t_1), \ldots, a(t_k))$ \hfill and f names a function on individuals

$a(P)$ is a set of k-tuples of \hfill where P is any k-ary
members of D \hfill predicate letter ($k \geq 1$)

a_w is the restriction of a to $d(w)$ on the above type of arguments and also satisfying the following:

---

[25] N.B. the assignment function is in effect doing the jobs of both an interpretation and a valuation. This rides roughshod over an important philosophical distinction in the interest of simplifying things in areas not of immediate concern to us (cf. Dunn and Hardegree 2001). In particular, since the assignment function is doing this double duty, '$*$' can do the duty of both an undefined truth value and an undefined member of a domain.

$$a_w(t) = \begin{cases} a(t) & \text{if } a(t) \in d(w), \text{ or} \\ & \text{if } a(t) = a(f(t_1, \ldots, t_k)) \\ & \quad \text{for some } t_1, \ldots, t_k \text{ s.t. } a(t_1), \ldots, a(t_k) \in d(w) \\ * & \text{otherwise} \end{cases}$$

$$a_w(s = t) = \begin{cases} \text{T} & \text{if } a_w(s) = a_w(t) \text{ and } a(s) \in d(w) \\ \text{F} & \text{if } a(s) \neq a(t) \text{ and } a(s), a(t) \in d(w) \\ * & \text{otherwise} \end{cases}$$

$$a_w(C_i(t)) = \begin{cases} \text{T} & \text{if } a(t) \in d(w') \text{ for all } w' \text{ such that } wR_iw' \\ \text{F} & \text{if } a(t) \in d(w) \\ & \quad \text{and } a(t) \notin d(w') \text{ for some } w' \text{ s.t. } wR_iw' \\ * & \text{otherwise} \end{cases}$$

For k-ary predicate letters P, other than equality and C_i (for $i = 1, \ldots, n$), we have

$$a_w(P(t_1, \ldots, t_k)) = \begin{cases} \text{T} & \text{if } a(t_1), \ldots, a(t_k) \in d(w) \\ & \quad \text{and } a(t_1, \ldots, t_k) \in a(P) \\ \text{F} & \text{if } a(t_1), \ldots, a(t_k) \in d(w) \\ & \quad \text{and } a(t_1, \ldots, t_k) \notin a(P) \\ * & \text{otherwise} \end{cases}$$

For an arbitrary sentence φ,

$$a_w(S_i\varphi) = \begin{cases} \text{T} & \text{if } a_{w'}(\varphi) = \text{T, for all } w' \text{ such that } wR_iw' \\ \text{F} & \text{if } a_{w'}(\varphi) \text{ is defined for all } w' \text{ such that } wR_iw' \\ & \quad \text{and } a_{w'}(\varphi) = \text{F for some } w' \text{ such that } wR_iw' \\ * & \text{otherwise} \end{cases}$$

$$a_w(\forall x\varphi) = \begin{cases} \text{T} & \text{if } a_w(\varphi[t/x]) = \text{T, for all } t \text{ s.t. } a(t) \in d(w) \\ \text{F} & \text{if } a_w(\varphi[t/x]) = \text{F, for some } t \text{ s.t. } a(t) \in d(w) \\ * & \text{otherwise} \end{cases}$$

where $\varphi[t/x]$ is the same sentence as φ except that all free occurrences of x in φ are replaced by t

$$a_w(\varphi \wedge \psi) = \begin{cases} \text{T} & \text{if } a_w(\varphi) = \text{T and } a_w(\psi) = \text{T} \\ \text{F} & \text{if } a_w(\varphi) = \text{F or } a_w(\psi) = \text{F} \\ & \quad \text{and both } a_w(\varphi) \text{ and } a_w(\psi) \text{ are defined} \\ * & \text{otherwise} \end{cases}$$

$$a_w(\varphi \vee \psi) = \begin{cases} T & \text{if } a_w(\varphi) = T \text{ or } a_w(\psi) = T \\ & \text{and both } a_w(\varphi) \text{ and } a_w(\psi) \text{ are defined} \\ F & \text{if } a_w(\varphi) = F \text{ and } a_w(\psi) = F \\ * & \text{otherwise} \end{cases}$$

$$a_w(\varphi \to \psi) = \begin{cases} T & \text{if } a_w(\varphi) = F \text{ or } a_w(\psi) = T \\ & \text{and both } a_w(\varphi) \text{ and } a_w(\psi) \text{ are defined} \\ F & \text{if } a_w(\varphi) = T \text{ and } a_w(\psi) = F \\ * & \text{otherwise} \end{cases}$$

$$a_w(\neg \varphi) = \begin{cases} T & \text{if } a_w(\varphi) = F \\ F & \text{if } a_w(\varphi) = T \\ * & \text{otherwise} \end{cases}$$

7.3 Axioms and Rules

It should be clear from the language set out above that the logic we are about to present will be a quantified modal logic. These are notoriously difficult semantically. In addition to the problems associated with modality per se, there are a number of problems associated with the interaction of modality and quantification.[26] I intend to skirt as many of these issues as I can that do not bear directly on our concerns. This leaves more than enough to discuss, which we will do as issues arise.

Axioms 1 through 5 are the universal closures of the following, where there are no freely occurring constant terms in α, β, or γ.

1. $\alpha \to (\beta \to \alpha)$
2. $(\alpha \to (\beta \to \gamma)) \to ((\alpha \to \beta) \to (\alpha \to \gamma))$
3. $(\neg \beta \to \neg \alpha) \to (\neg \beta \to (\alpha \to \beta))$
4. $S_i(\alpha) \wedge S_i(\alpha \to \beta) \to S_i(\beta)$
5. $S_i(\alpha) \to \alpha$

The reason for the restrictions on axioms 1 through 5 is to make sure that they are true in all models. Without the restrictions, an axiom would not have a defined truth value at a world if it contained a term that failed to denote there. While the idea of axioms that are not necessarily true at all worlds is somewhat bizarre, there is no harm in it; however, for convenience and to avoid unnecessary confusion, we adopt the above restrictions. We also have the following axioms concerning identity:

6. $\forall x(x = x)$

---

[26] Some of the major issues are discussed in Garson 1984.

7. $\forall x \forall y ((x = y) \to (\varphi \to \varphi'))$

   (where φ' is the result of replacing no, some or all occurrences of 'x' in φ with 'y', and where neither φ nor φ' contain any free occurrences of any constant terms)

The logical rules are as follows:

R1. (Modus Ponens) From φ and $\varphi \to \psi$ infer ψ.

R2. (Epistemic Generalization) From $\vdash \varphi$ infer $\vdash S_i\varphi$ (for $i = 1,\ldots,n$).

R3. (Universal Instantiation) From $\forall x\varphi \wedge Mt$ infer $\varphi[t/x]$.

   (for any term t, where φ is a sentence in the language, and $\varphi[t/x]$ is the same sentence as φ except that all free occurrences of x in φ are replaced by t)

R4. (Universal Generalization) From $\psi \to (Mt \to \varphi)$ infer $\psi \to \forall x\varphi[x/t]$.

   (where t is any term that does not occur freely in ψ or in any assumption on which $\psi \to (Mt \to \varphi)$ depends)

R5. (Knowledge Relation) From $S_i\varphi$ infer $C_i t$.

   (where φ is an arbitrary sentence and t is any term occurring freely in φ)

Presumably, modus ponens requires no comment other than that φ and ψ may be either closed or open. Epistemic generalization will be discussed briefly below and more extensively in the next chapter. The quantification rules, **R3** and **R4**, are what distinguish this as a free logic. ('$\exists x$' is taken as the standard notational abbreviation for '$\neg \forall x \neg$'.)

7.4 Metalogic

To describe or metalogical results we need to adopt the following notational conventions. Let Γ stand for a finite set of sentences and φ, ψ, etc. stand for arbitrary sentences as before. '$\Gamma \vdash \varphi$' means that φ is derivable from Γ and the axioms using the inference rules of the logic. '$\Gamma \models \varphi$' means that, in all models, φ is true at all the worlds at which all the members of Γ are true. The more standard notation corresponding to our '$\models$' is '$\models$'. But, this notation is usually assigned double duty. It is used in the way we have used '$\models$', and it is used to mean that a formula is true at a particular world or in a particular model. The reason for this is unclear; however, part of the justification may stem from the following. To represent that a formula φ is true at all worlds in all models we usually write '$\models \varphi$'. But, a logic and semantics are generally designed so that axioms are true at all worlds in all models. (After all, these formulae are *axioms*.) Thus, if Γ is the set of axioms, it is somewhat redundant to write '$\Gamma \models \varphi$' since the axioms are true in all the models. Thus, the two uses coincide for logical truths. This confusion of notation is thus somewhat forgivable. But, we will presently look at a logic in which the coincidence between the two uses is even less: we will consider possibilities in which some individuals may not know all of the axioms. This means that some of them may not be true at all of the possible worlds. To keep this clear we have adopted the above usage of '$\models$'. Nonetheless, since in our present system and semantics axioms are true at all worlds in all models, we will write '$\models \varphi$' to represent logical truths and '$\vdash \varphi$' to represent theorems. This notational point out of the way, we begin to address soundness, our first result.

Soundness

Theorem 6 (Soundness) *If $\Gamma \vdash \varphi$, then $\Gamma \models \varphi$.*

Proof. This proof is fairly standard and trivial. To begin we need the following lemma.

Lemma 7 *All axioms are valid in all models.*

Proof. This result follows directly by inspection of the assignment function. □

We now proceed to prove the theorem by showing that all the ways that φ can follow from Γ are ways that preserve truth.

- **φ is an axiom or member of Γ.** Then $\Gamma \models \varphi$ trivially.
- **φ is obtained by modus ponens from ψ and $\psi \to \varphi$.** This follows by a trivial argument via strong induction and by the definition of the assignment function. Suppose that soundness holds for all lines of a derivation up to the one in question, where φ occurs. Then, by inductive hypothesis, $\Gamma \models \psi$ and $\Gamma \models \psi \to \varphi$. So, clearly $\Gamma \models \varphi$ by the definition of the assignment function.
- **φ is obtained by epistemic generalization.** Then φ is $S_i\psi$ for some i and some ψ. Proceeding again by induction, we have $\Gamma \models \psi$. Since it must be the case that $\vdash \psi$, by inductive hypothesis, $\models \psi$. So ψ is true at all worlds, hence true at all worlds accessible for i from any given world, i.e., $\models S_i\psi$. Thus, a fortiori $\Gamma \models S_i\psi$.
- **φ is obtained by universal instantiation.** Then φ is of the form $\psi[t/x]$. Proceeding by induction, we assume $\Gamma \models \forall x \psi \wedge Mt$. So, $\Gamma \models \forall x \psi$ and $\Gamma \models Mt$. If x does not occur freely in ψ, then $\forall x \psi$ is true iff ψ is true, and ψ is $\psi[t/x]$ in this case. So $\Gamma \models \psi[t/x]$.

If x does occur freely in ψ, then $\Gamma \models \psi[t/x]$ by the definition of the assignment function.

φ **is obtained by universal generalization.** So, φ is of the form $\psi \to \forall x \theta[x/t]$, and, by inductive hypothesis, $\Gamma \models \psi \to Mt \to \theta$ where t is an arbitrary term not occurring freely in ψ or any member of Γ. We may assume $\Gamma \models \psi$. (If ψ is false, the result is trivial. And, if ψ is undefined, by inductive hypothesis, all of Γ is undefined and again the result is trivial.) So, by definition of the assignment function, $\Gamma \models \psi \to \forall x \theta[x/t]$.

φ **is obtained by knowledge relation.** This rule can be seen to be truth preserving simply by inspecting the assignment function. $\square$

Completeness

Theorem 8 (Completeness) *If* $\Gamma \models \varphi$, *then* $\Gamma \vdash \varphi$.

Proof. We give a Henkin style proof for the completeness of the logic. That is, we construct a model where the worlds are maximal consistent sets of sentences and show that every consistent set is satisfiable. (This is equivalent to completeness by the following argument: Restricting ourselves to the maximal consistent sets containing Γ, if $\Gamma \cup \{\varphi\}$ is valid in a set of worlds, then $\Gamma \cup \{\neg \varphi\}$ is not simultaneously satisfiable in any member of that set. Assuming Γ itself is consistent, if $\Gamma \cup \{\neg \varphi\}$ is inconsistent, it can only be because $\Gamma \vdash \varphi$. Thus, if we can prove that the inconsistency of $\Gamma \cup \{\neg \varphi\}$ follows from its failure to be simultaneously satisfiable, we will have shown completeness. We do this by proving the contrapositive, i.e., that every consistent set is satisfiable.)

We now take an arbitrary consistent set of sentences and show that it is satisfiable. Assume that we have a set of sentences Γ that is consistent with respect to the logic, By Lindenbaum's Lemma, this can be extended to a maximal consistent set v in some language L.[27] Unfortunately, the basic Lindenbaum result does not guarantee quite enough. In order to prove what we want we must construct our maximal consistent sets so that the following condition is satisfied.

ω-completeness: If $w \vdash Mt \to \varphi$ for every term t of L, then $w \vdash \forall x \varphi[x/t]$.

Note that this is equivalent to:

If $w \cup \{\neg \forall x \varphi\}$ is consistent, then for some term t of L, $w \cup \{\neg(Mt \to \varphi[t/x])\}$ is consistent.

---

[27] Cf., e.g., Chellas 1980 for a statement and proof of Lindenbaum's Lemma (including an account of the Lindenbauming procedure).

We say that an ω-complete, maximal consistent set of sentences of L is saturated (for L). To produce a saturated set, we proceed by Lindenbauming and show that our construction satisfies the equivalent formulation of ω-completeness. Begin with a consistent set Γ, of sentences in L. Order all sentences of L, $\{A_1, A_2, A_3, \ldots\}$. Then, define a series of sets $M_0 = \Gamma, M_1, M_2, \ldots$ by letting $M_{i+1} = M_i \cup \{A_{i+1}\}$ if doing so leaves M_{i+1} consistent. Otherwise $M_{i+1} = M_i$. The union of the M_i's is maximally consistent by Lindenbaum's Lemma. To ensure ω-completeness we modify the construction slightly. If A_{i+1} is $\neg \forall x \varphi$ and $M_i \cup \{A_{i+1}\}$ is consistent, then we let $M_{i+1} = M_i \cup \{A_{i+1}, \neg(Mt \to \varphi[t/x])\}$ where t is a term foreign to $M_i \cup \{A_{i+1}\}$. We claim that M_{i+1} is consistent if $M_i \cup \{A_{i+1}\}$ is consistent. If not, then it must be the case that $M_i \cup \{A_{i+1}\} \vdash Mt \to \varphi[t/x]$. Since t does not occur in $M_i \cup \{A_{i+1}\}$, we can apply universal generalization to this in order to get that $M_i \cup \{A_{i+1}\} \vdash \forall x \varphi$. But then, $M_i \cup \{A_{i+1}\}$ is inconsistent. Contradiction. This construction preserves consistency and guarantees both maximality and ω-completeness.

We now proceed to the construction of the canonical model. Again, starting with a consistent set Γ of sentences of L, we extend this to a saturated set v by means of the above procedure. Now, consider a language L^* containing infinitely more terms than L. We define the canonical model, $\langle W, R_1, \ldots R_n, D, d, a \rangle$, as follows. Let W be the set of all sets w of sentences satisfying the following:

1. Each world w is a saturated set for a language L_w, and L_w is a sublanguage of L^* such that there are infinitely many terms of L^* not occurring in L_w.
2. $v \in W$.
3. For all terms s and t that are member of both L_w and $L_{w'}$, $s = t \in w$ iff $s = t \in w'$.
4. If $P(t_1, \ldots, t_k)$ is an expression of both L_w and $L_{w'}$, then $P(t_1, \ldots, t_k) \in w$ iff $P(t_1, \ldots, t_k) \in w'$.

Clauses 3 and 4 force agreement between worlds with regard to the membership of certain sentences. Clause 2 is present simply to ensure that other worlds accommodate to v in such agreement.

The assignment function for terms is given by $a(t) = \{s : s = t \in \bigcup W\}$.

For an arbitrary k-ary predicate letter P, the assignment function is given by $a(P) = \{\langle t_1, \ldots, t_k \rangle : P(t_1, \ldots, t_k) \in \bigcup W\}$.

Definition of the assignment function for other arguments is as usual.

86 / Logic, Convention, and Common Knowledge

The domain is given by $D = \bigcup_{w \in W} \{a(t) : t \in L_w\}$, and thus $d(w) = \{a(t) : t \in L_w\}$.

For each i, wR_iw' iff $S_i\varphi \in w \Rightarrow \varphi \in w'$.

With the specification of the canonical model finished we proceed to the main step in our completeness proof, the truth lemma.

Lemma 9 *If φ is a sentence of L_w, then $a_w(\varphi) = T$ iff $\varphi \in w$.*

Proof. The proof proceeds by cases.

Case i: (φ **is of the form** $\psi \wedge \theta$, $\psi \vee \theta$, $\psi \to \theta$, **or** $\neg \psi$) All of these follow by trivial inductive arguments.

Case ii: (φ **is of the form** $s = t$) If $s = t \in w$, then $s \in L_w$ and $t \in L_w$. So, $a(s) \in d(w)$ and $a(t) \in d(w)$. We need that $a(s) = a(t)$. Suppose $u \in a(s)$. Then $u = s \in w'$ for some w'. Consider a language L_{w^+} formed by adding u to L_w (together with all resulting expressions). There exists a saturated set of sentences of L_{w^+}, w^+, containing $u = t$. So, $a(s) = a(t)$ and $a_w(s = t) = T$. If $a_w(s = t) = T$, then $a(s), a(t) \in d(w)$ and $a(s) = a(t)$. So, $s, t \in L_w$. Since w is maximal consistent, $s = t \in w$ or $s \neq t \in w$. But, if $a(s) = a(t)$, there is some world in W, containing $s = t$. Thus, by clause 3 of the definition of W, $s = t \in w$.

Case iii: (φ **is of the form** $C_i t$) If $C_i t \in w$, then, by maximal consistency, either $S_i(t = t) \in w$ or $\neg S_i(t = t) \in w$. We will see in case **v** below that if $\neg S_i(t = t) \in w$, then $t \neq t \in w'$ for some w' such that wR_iw', which is impossible. Thus, $S_i(t = t) \in w$. Therefore, $t = t \in w'$ for all w' such that wR_iw'. So, $a(t) \in d(w')$ for all w' such that wR_iw', and $a_w(C_i t) = T$. If $C_i t \notin w$, then by knowledge relation and the maximal consistency of w, $S_i\psi \notin w$ for any sentence ψ containing any occurrences of t. In particular, $S_i(t = t) \notin w$. And, as we have already mentioned, this leads to a contradiction.

Case iv: (φ **is of the form** $P(t_1, \ldots, t_k)$) If $P(t_1, \ldots, t_k) \in w$, then $a(\langle t_i, \ldots, t_k \rangle) \in a(P)$ and $a(t_1), \ldots, a(t_k) \in d(w)$. But, $a(\langle t_i, \ldots, t_k \rangle) \in a(P)$, and $a(t_1), \ldots, a(t_k) \in d(w)$ iff $a_w(P(t_1, \ldots, t_k)) = T$. If $P(t_1, \ldots, t_k) \notin w$, then $\neg P(t_1, \ldots, t_k) \in w$. Thus, by clause 4 of the definition of W, $a(\langle t_1, \ldots, t_k \rangle) \notin a(P)$. So, $a_w(P(t_1, \ldots, t_k)) \neq T$.

Case v: (φ **is of the form** $S_i\psi$) If $S_i\psi \in w$, then $\psi \in w'$ for all w' such that wR_iw' iff $a_{w'}(\psi) = T$ for all such w'. Thus, $a_w(S_i\psi) = T$. If $S_i\psi \notin w$, then $\neg S_i\psi \in w$. We claim that if $\neg S_i\psi \in w$, then there is a $w' \in W$ such that wR_iw' and $\neg\psi \in w'$. To show this, assume that $\neg S_i\psi \in w$ and let $\delta = \{\varphi : S_i\varphi \in w\} \cup \{\neg\psi\}$. It is easy to see that δ is consistent and contains only terms of L_w. It is not clear that there are infinitely many terms of L_w foreign to δ. Thus, it is not clear that δ can be extended to a saturated set of sentences for L_w. Let A be the set of terms occurring in L^* but not in L_w. We can use A to extend δ to a saturated set, but that might not be in W because it might not have infinitely many terms of L^* foreign to it. We solve this by partitioning A into two infinite sets, A_1 and A_2. We then use A_1 to extend δ to a saturated set w', and keep A_2 to ensure that there are infinitely many terms of L^* foreign to $L_{w'}$. To establish the claim it remains only to show that wR_iw', but this follows trivially from the composition of δ. With the claim thus shown, it follows by inductive hypothesis, that if $S_i\psi \notin w$, then $a_w(S_i\psi) \neq \mathrm{T}$.

Case vi: (φ **is of the form** $\forall x\psi$) By universal instantiation and ω-completeness, $\forall x\psi \in w$ is equivalent to $\psi[t/x] \in w$ for all t in L_w. But, by inductive hypothesis, this is equivalent to $a_w(\psi[t/x]) = \mathrm{T}$ for all t in L_w. And, by the definition of d, this is equivalent to $a_w(\psi[t/x]) = \mathrm{T}$ for all t such that $a(t) \in d(w)$, which is equivalent to $a_w(\forall x\psi) = \mathrm{T}$.

□

Now that we have established the truth lemma, completeness follows immediately since we have shown that Γ (an arbitrary consistent set of sentences) is satisfied by the canonical model.

□

7.5 Some Metalogical Corollaries

Corollary 10 *The deduction theorem fails to hold for this logic.*

Proof. This becomes obvious when we look at our rule of universal instantiation. From $\forall x\varphi \wedge Mt$ we can infer $\varphi[t/x]$. However, from $\forall x\varphi$ we cannot infer $Mt \rightarrow \varphi[t/x]$, for if t fails to denote, $Mt \rightarrow \varphi[t/x]$ will have an undefined truth value. So, for example, $\forall x(x = x)$ is an axiom and thus true at all worlds. If the deduction theorem were to hold, then we could conclude from universal instantiation and completeness that $Mt \rightarrow (t = t)$ is true at all worlds. But, this is clearly undefined at any world where t fails to denote. □

If we assume that all terms denote everywhere, we can prove a fairly standard first order deduction theorem. However, such a restriction would remove most—if not all— of the interesting innovations of our logic. Basically, the absence of a deduction theorem means that the logic does not have enough expressive power to capture its own consequence relation. While somewhat surprising there is no cause for concern, especially when we realize that this limitation applies only in those cases where one literally does not know what one is talking about. As we will discuss in the next chapter, ours is a logic of epistemic, not alethic, modalities.

Corollary 11 *The Carnap-Barcan Formula (CBF) does not hold in this logic.*

Proof.
CBF refers to all formulae of the form $\forall x S_i(\varphi(x))) \to S_i(\forall x \varphi(x))$. To see that it does not hold, consider a world w such that $w \models \forall x S_i(C_i x)$. In other words, given any constant t that denotes at w, individual i knows t (at w), and he knows that he knows t. But, he need not also know that he knows *all* the individuals that denote at w. To be slightly more rigorous, consider a model with three worlds, w_1, w_2, w_3, such that $w_n R_i w_m$ iff $n \leq m$. Let t denote at all three worlds, and let s denote only at w_2. Then, $w_1 \models \forall x S_i(C_i x)$ since t is the only term to which x can be instantiated and it denotes everywhere. But, $w_1 \not\models S_i(\forall x C_i x)$. To see this note that w_2 is accessible from w_1, but $w_2 \not\models \forall x C_i x$ because s denotes at w_2 but not at w_3. Thus, CBF must not be valid. Thus, by soundness, CBF is not a theorem of the logic. □

As a similar trivillary, we have

Corollary 12 *The converse of the Carnap-Barcan Formula (CCBF) does not hold in this logic.*

Proof. CCBF refers to all formulae of the form $S_i(\forall x \varphi(x)) \to \forall x S_i(\varphi(x)))$. By epistemic generalization, since $\forall x(x = x)$ is a theorem, so is $S_i(\forall x(x = x))$. In particular, these theorems are true at all worlds in a model with exactly two worlds, w_1, w_2, both R_i-accessible from each other, at one of which t denotes and at the other of which it does not. If CCBF were valid, it would follow that $\forall x S_i(x = x)$ is valid. Then, if t were to denote at world w_1, $S_i(t = t)$ would be true at w_1. But, this would mean that t would have to denote at w_2. But, t cannot denote at both w_1 and w_2. And, since w_1 was arbitrarily chosen to have t denote, $\forall x S_i(x = x)$ cannot be valid in this model. Thus, CCBF must not be valid, hence not a theorem. □

Given our world relative domains these last two corollaries should be no surprise (Hughes and Cresswell 1968, pp. 170–ff.). The desirability of CBF and its converse has been the subject of some controversy (*ibid.*). This has been essentially focussed, however, on alethic modalities. In our context it is fairly clear that the results are as we would want them to be. With respect to CCBF, the formula we chose to prove invalidity makes this obvious. We want to differentiate a desirable understanding of identity from a familiarity with any given individual. With respect to CBF, we have the informal explanation we gave in the proof. If this is not obvious enough, consider the following situation of someone at a party. Suppose that he in fact knows all of the people at the party. But, there are a lot of people there, and he hasn't paid attention to whether he's seen everyone there or not. So even though he knows everyone there and even knows of each of them that he knows them, he doesn't know that he knows *everyone* there. He is willing to countenance that there is someone at the party whom he has never met. If CBF were a logical truth for us, this situation would be a logical impossibility. Whenever one knew all the individuals in a situation, one would also have to know that those were all of them. But, this is not generally epistemically justified.

8

Three Grades of Epistemic Involvement

> If I see the tallest spy hide a letter under a rock, then there is a clear sense in which I have the information that the tallest spy has hidden the letter. However, if I don't know that he is a spy, say, then I don't know that the tallest spy has hidden a letter. Information travels at the speed of logic, genuine knowledge travels only at the speed of cognition and inference. Put another way, I would argue that much of the work in logic of knowledge is best understood in terms of the logic of information. Put more positively, I think that a theory of information should be a part of logic, but I doubt that the theory of knowledge really is.
>
> —Jon Barwise in "On the Model Theory of Common Knowledge"

Epistemic logic in the tradition of Hintikka (1962) generally fails to be cognitive in the sense mentioned in the above quote. The logic set out in the last chapter is more of a true epistemic logic in the area of individual constants and quantification. In that logic, a subject can only say meaningful things using constant terms that are meaningful to that subject. However, the rule of epistemic generalization, a feature that it shares with most epistemic logics, runs contrary to the basic nature of knowledge that we would like to capture. The logic of the next chapter is still more epistemic in this regard. We now consider these and other technical and philosophical aspects of the logic of familiarity given in the last chapter and of the logic of awareness given in the next chapter.

8.1 Knowledge Predicates

One important question about the mechanisms we have set out for knowledge representation is whether or not we need the knowledge predicates (C predicates) as primitives at all. Is there not some way that we can define them in terms of the, more traditional, knowledge operators? Obvious candidates for defining $C_i t$ are $S_i(Mt)$ and $\exists x S_i(x = t)$. The latter of these is of course the classic definition from Hintikka (1962, sections 6.6–ff.). Any debate on which of these is more appropriate is forestalled by their equivalence in the above semantics and is a fortiori precluded once we realize that neither can ever be false. In any given world, they are both either true or undefined. Nonetheless, perhaps this indicates not the indispensability of the knowledge predicates but the inadequacy of the assignment function.

Perhaps the assignment function makes unnecessary distinctions in the case of the knowledge predicates. The criteria for an assignment of T may be straightforward enough: to be known a term must be present at all accessible worlds. But what about the distinction between being assigned F and being undefined? Recall that ours is a logic of epistemic, not alethic, modalities. If 'Pegasus' does not denote at a world, it doesn't just mean that he doesn't exist there; it means that he is not known there. So, an atomic sentence that contains a term that fails to denote at a world should fail to have a truth value there. This explains the conditions under which $a_w(C_i t)$ is undefined. What about falsity? Let C_a be the knowledge predicate for Abbey. Then, from Abbey's perspective $C_a t$ should never be false. How could she fail to know the reference of a term that she can knowingly use to refer correctly? So, $C_a t$ should only be false for someone other than Abbey.

We may not have considered deep enough modifications to the assignment function. Let us consider a different approach to semantic models.[28] In place of our world relative domains we assume one constant domain, D. And, instead of having only rigid designators, we allow possibly nonrigid designators. In other words, it is possible for $a_w(t)$ and $a_{w'}(t)$ to pick out different individuals. This is so even if one of these worlds is accessible from the other. This will of course affect the entire assignment function; however, we need not consider the details of this. We can restrict our attention to quantification and to the C predicates. Thus, in place of our current assignment function for quantification we have

$$a_w(\forall x \varphi) = \begin{cases} T & \text{if } a_w|_x^d(\varphi) = T, \text{ for all } d \in D \\ F & \text{if } a_w|_x^d(\varphi) = F, \text{ for some } d \in D \end{cases}$$

where $a_w|_x^d$ is the same assignment function as a_w except that it assigns d to x.

---

[28] This approach to defining the C predicates was pointed out to me by Martín Abadi in a personal communication. On reflection, it is basically an approach described in chapter 6 of Hintikka 1962.

Once we have done this, we can make the following definition.

$$C_i(t) =_{df} \exists x(S_i(t = x))$$

This definition is no longer trivial in the sense of being always true or meaningless. So, with a modified semantics we can eliminate the knowledge predicates as primitives.

Let us consider what we have done in order to make the knowledge predicates eliminable. Looking first at the semantic level, we have done two things: we replaced our world relative domains with constant ones, and we allowed nonrigid designators. The first of these changes has the effect of making our worlds metaphysical, rather than epistemic, entities. With world relative domains, possible worlds can be thought of as different ways that individuals might consider the world to be. With constant domains, they are instead different ways the world might be, ways that individuals may or may not distinguish. This makes knowledge a, perhaps restricted, form of alethic modality. This in turn makes our epistemic decisions beholden to metaphysical decisions in an odd way. It makes some metaphysical sense to say that we can't talk about what is known until we have decided what there is to know. But, it makes epistemological sense to say that deciding what there is to know is ultimately limited by what is known. When reasoning about knowledge, to start out reasoning in terms of alethic rather than epistemic possibility is to start out on the wrong foot. We will return to this point below. Another problem with constant domains is that it makes it impossible for one world to be contained in another. This will be crucial to our characterization of common knowledge. Given these considerations, the semantics that we are interested in must have world relative domains.

The other change that we made to allow the knowledge predicates to be eliminably defined was to allow nonrigid designators. One affect of this change is to render invalid the knowledge relation rule. To see this suppose that $S_i(Pt \vee \neg Pt)$ is true at w. Since t need not be assigned the same value at all worlds accessible (for i) from w, $\exists x(S_i(x = t))$ may be false at w. Thus, there is a formula, φ, containing the constant term t such that $S_i\varphi$ is true but $C_i t$ is false at w. So, the knowledge relation rule is lost by allowing nonrigid designators. Perhaps this is not a bad thing. Perhaps knowledge relation makes a logic that is unrealistically strong. But, knowledge relation is actually a form of limitation on knowledge. In order to know a formula one must know all the singular terms that are in it. This seems to be overly restrictive. One should not need to know t in order to know that $\neg(Pt \wedge \neg Pt)$. Similar considerations were largely responsible for motivating free logic. But, the essence

94 / Logic, Convention, and Common Knowledge

of this can be preserved without eliminating the knowledge relation rule. The logical motivation for wanting to make $\neg(Pt \land \neg Pt)$ known in no way derives from the constant term contained therein. Thus, what we are actually motivated to claim is something like $\vdash S_i(\forall x \neg(Px \land \neg Px))$. But, this is actually a theorem even though $\not\vdash S_i(\neg(Pt \land \neg Pt))$. In order to instantiate the variable we must know to what we are instantiating. To insist that $S_i(\neg(Pt \land \neg Pt))$ be true even if $C_i t$ is false is to allow t to function as a variable while masquerading as a constant term. The sort of restriction that the knowledge relation rule imposes is actually desirable. It seems that our knowledge predicates are only eliminable as primitives at the expense of rendering our logic less epistemic.

Before leaving the topic of the knowledge relation rule we note that its desirable features are not limited to logical truths. It is similarly reasonable with respect to contingent formulae. For example, we can satisfy $S_i(\exists x(C_j x \land \neg C_i x))$ in our original semantics. This may seem rather surprising given the example using 'Abbey' several paragraphs above. To see this result consider two worlds w and w' such that each is accessible from itself with respect to R_i and R_j, and each is (only) R_i-accessible from the other. Suppose that s exists only at w and that t exists only at w'. Then, at both w and w' there is an individual that is known to j but not to i, and i knows this.

8.2 Representing Knowing Situations

In this section we will attempt to add machinery to what has been developed above that will allow us to syntactically capture common knowledge. Ultimately we will not succeed in using our current semantic framework for that purpose, and this particular approach will be abandoned. Familiarity alone is simply not a sufficient ground for common knowledge. Nonetheless, the attempt itself is instructive. In the next chapter we will develop an adequate framework.

We begin by looking at some additions to the language and interpret them in the existing semantics. In order to syntactically represent common knowledge we will have to expand the language somewhat. The first expansion is rather trivial. Amongst the individual constant symbols: $a, b, c, \ldots$ we distinguish a set of situation constants referring to situations (possible worlds): $w_1, w_2, w_3, \ldots$ These may stand in all the places where ordinary constants go. The assignment function remains the same. In particular, the assignment function for the C-predicates remains unchanged. Thus, that individual i is familiar with situation w is represented '$C_i w$'. We also distinguish amongst the individual variables a set of variables that can only be instantiated with situation constants: $z_1, z_2, z_3, \ldots$.

Recall the shared-situation account of common knowledge from chapter 4. A and B have common knowledge that φ just in case there is a situation w such that:

- $w \models \varphi$
- $w \models A$ knows w.
- $w \models B$ knows w.

In our semantics we have given a characterization of what we mean by $w \models \varphi$. Did we also set out what we mean by 'A knows w.'? It might seem so since this is the ordinary language way of writing '$C_a w$'. But, this is not what we mean by 'A knows w.' By this we mean to express more than A's mere familiarity with w. If A and B are familiar with some situation w in which Adlai Stevenson is president, they can still both believe that they are not in situation w. Neither of them would then even believe that Stevenson is president much less that they have common knowledge that he is president. It is not enough that they be familiar with w; they must also believe that they are in w. As we stated in chapter 4, the idea is that, in situation w, they each know that w is the situation. This is what we need to set out.

The first thing that we will need in order to accomplish this is a way to use '$\models$' on the syntactic level. We thus add to the language in the following manner. If 'w' is a situation constant and 'φ' is any formula, then '$w \models \varphi$' is a formula. We extend the assignment function to deal with these formulae as follows:

$$a_w(w' \models \varphi) = \begin{cases} T & \text{if } w' \in d(w) \text{ and } a_{w'}(\varphi) = T \\ F & \text{if } w' \in d(w) \text{ and } a_{w'}(\varphi) = F, \text{ or} \\ & \text{if } w' \in d(w), a_w(\varphi) \text{ is defined and } a_{w'}(\varphi) = * \\ * & \text{otherwise} \end{cases}$$

What does it mean to say that someone knows that a situation w is the situation, i.e., that the situation w obtains? We propose the following semantic characterization.

$$a_w(S_i(w')) = T \text{ iff } a_w(S_i(\varphi)) = T \text{ and } a_w(S_i(w' \models \varphi)) = T \text{ for all } \varphi$$
$$\text{such that } a_{w'}(\varphi) = T$$

This of course requires that we add to the language sentences of the form $S_i(w)$ where 'w' is a situation constant. The assignment function for these formulae is given as follows:

96 / LOGIC, CONVENTION, AND COMMON KNOWLEDGE

$$a_w(S_i w') = \begin{cases} T & a_w(S_i(w' \models \varphi)) = T \text{ and } a_w(S_i(\varphi)) = T \\ & \text{for all } \varphi \text{ s.t. } a_{w'}(\varphi) = T \\ F & a_w(S_i(w' \models \varphi)) = T \\ & \text{and } a_w(S_i(\varphi)) \neq T \text{ for some } \varphi \text{ s.t. } a_{w'}(\varphi) = T \\ * & \text{otherwise} \end{cases}$$

In order to understand this it is helpful to set out the assignment for formulae of the form $S_i(w \models \varphi)$. Given the above characterization of '$\models$', these are given as follows:

$$a_w(S_i(w' \models \varphi)) = \begin{cases} T & \text{if for all } w'' \text{ s.t. } wR_i w'', w' \in d(w'') \\ & \text{and } a_{w'}(\varphi) = T \\ F & \text{if for all } w'' \text{ s.t. } wR_i w'', a_{w''}(w' \models \varphi) \text{ is} \\ & \text{defined, and there is a } w'' \text{ s.t. } wR_i w'', \\ & \text{and s.t. } a_{w''}(w' \models \varphi) = F \\ * & \text{otherwise} \end{cases}$$

This can be rewritten as

$$a_w(S_i(w' \models \varphi)) = \begin{cases} T & \text{if } a_w(C_i w') = T \text{ and } a_{w'}(\varphi) = T \\ F & \text{if } a_w(C_i w') = T \text{ and } a_w(S_i(\varphi \vee \neg \varphi)) = T \\ & \text{and } a_{w'}(\varphi) \neq T \\ * & \text{otherwise} \end{cases}$$

We can thus rewrite the definition of the assignment function for $S_i(w')$ as

$$a_w(S_i w') = \begin{cases} T & \text{if } a_w(C_i w') = T \\ & \text{and } (a_{w'}(\varphi) = T \Rightarrow a_w(S_i(\varphi)) = T) \\ F & \text{if } a_w(C_i w') = T \text{ and, for some } \varphi \text{ s.t. } a'_w(\varphi) = T, \\ & a_w(S_i(\varphi)) \neq T \\ * & \text{otherwise} \end{cases}$$

Thus, in English, 'Eleri knows that w' obtains.' is true at w if (at w) she is familiar with w' and if whenever a formula is true at w', it is a formula she knows to be true (at w). 'Eleri knows that w' obtains.' is false at w if (at w) she is familiar with w', but there is some sentence that is true at w' that she does not know to be true (at w).

8.3 Representing Common Knowledge

These linguistic additions out of the way, we are now ready to define common knowledge. That agents i and j have common knowledge of φ, written '$S_{ij}\varphi$', is defined as follows:

$$S_{ij}\varphi \leftrightarrow \exists w(S_iw \wedge S_jw \wedge w \models S_iw \wedge w \models S_jw \wedge w \models \varphi)$$

Linguistic representations of common knowledge are not new (Halpern and Moses 1990, 1992). But, there are some new aspects to our definition. First, ours is an eliminable syntactic definition. Halpern and Moses defined common knowledge in terms of an infinite conjunction of expressions. Thus, common knowledge is not linguistically expressible for them in terms of the knowledge of the agents unless they expand their language to allow infinitary expressions. (Recall our discussion in section 4.2 about finite and infinite representations of common knowledge.) Also, our definition is for a first order language while theirs is for a propositional language. In addition we have given a syntactic characterization of the shared situation account of common knowledge. This was previously done by Barwise (1989b), but the language given therein was second order. We will say more about the relation between that characterization and ours in the next chapter.

This definition also accords better with certain intuitive differences between knowledge and common knowledge. Most epistemic logics are at least as strong as **S4**; thus, knowing that φ logically implies knowing that knowing that φ. This includes within the logic a self awareness that is not clearly always warranted. Nonetheless, as pointed out by Harman (1977, p. 423) and Barwise (1989a, p. 203), it does seem that common knowledge that φ should imply common knowledge of common knowledge that φ, etc.

We have not given any axioms or rules for common knowledge, but a moment's reflection tells us that positive introspection (the **4** axiom) is valid for common knowledge of φ provided that φ has a definite truth value. In fact, if instead of the axiom we have an inference rule, from $S_{ij}\varphi$ derive $S_{ij}S_{ij}\varphi$, we get a rule that is truth preserving for all φ in the language. Some feel that positive introspection is a reasonable theorem even for knowledge, but, negative introspection (theoremhood for sentences of the form '$\neg S_i\varphi \to S_i\neg S_i\varphi$') is generally viewed with as much suspicion as logical omniscience. (Recall that negative introspection is what is historically known as the **5** axiom.) Negative introspection is so-called because it states that for everything someone doesn't actually know, he knows that he doesn't know it. Unlike the case with axiom **4**, this caution is most reasonably carried over to common knowledge as well. The only case for which negative introspection seems reasonable is one in which the situation and proposition in question are known to the agents, but they don't know that the proposition is true. For example, if w is the situation and φ the proposition, then $S_{ij}w$ and

$S_{ij}\psi$, where ψ is $\varphi \vee \neg\varphi$.

The semantics we have given to our new expressions is intuitively appealing; nonetheless, the assignments we described create a technical difficulty. It is clear that for the language and semantics set out in above there are $2^{\aleph_0}$ worlds. Since we now are able to refer to worlds explicitly in our language, we must either expand to an uncountable language or explain our restriction to a countable one. At the least, a move to an uncountable language would complicate the completeness proof. But to base this decision on technical convenience is to punt away the intuitive appeal we desire. The situation is actually even worse than this however. For, if we retain the semantics we have given for formulae of the form '$S_i w$', our truth conditions are not wellfounded and cannot be given inductively in the usual manner. We will see below that what suffers from intuitive and philosophical difficulties is actually our attempt to use the current semantics to capture knowledge that a situation obtains, hence common knowledge. The semantics that we will motivate in its stead is fortuitously free of the above technical problems as well.

8.4 Familiarity and Knowledge Reconsidered

We have introduced epistemic predicates to indicate familiarity, to indicate that, e.g., James knows Eleri. We interpreted these by having world relative domains in our semantics, so that James knows Eleri precisely when Eleri is present in all the situations of which James can conceive. This semantics does quite well in capturing familiarity, but it gives up some standard features of semantics for epistemic logics. For example, suppose we want to represent that James does not know that Eleri is at preschool (even though he knows Eleri). On the usual understanding of knowledge in possible world semantics, we do this by having a world accessible to James from the real world in which Eleri is at preschool and one thus accessible in which she is not. If we represent that Eleri is at preschool in our language by Pe, then we would need to have worlds w and w' such that $a_w(Pe) = \text{T}$ and $a_{w'}(Pe) = \text{F}$. But, in our semantics either $a(e) \in a(P)$ or $a(e) \notin a(P)$. And, if the former, then at no world can F be assigned to Pe. And, if the latter, then at no world can T be assigned to Pe. So, either a_w or $a_{w'}$ as just given is spurious. What this means is that in our semantics, once we make a decision about what the (actual?) values of our syntactic expressions are, the only definite truth value a formula can receive at any possible world is one that agrees with these values. The only exception, where any flexibility in this regard is visible, is in the case of formulae involving the epistemic predicates. For, in that case truth values at a world are determined by the domains at that world and at worlds accessible from it—not just whether or not the formula is defined but also what the truth value is.

One conclusion that might be drawn from this observation is that we don't have an epistemic/modal logic at all. Once a subject is familiar with all the constant terms, the logic behaves classically. In fact, the above discussion amounts to an informal proof for any formula φ and world w that

if $w \models C_i(t)$ for all t occurring freely in φ, then $w \models S_i(\varphi) \leftrightarrow \varphi$.

The modality introduced in this logic is not one of knowing in the sense of being able to differentiate truth from falsehood (except in the case of statements claiming knowledge of certain individuals). Rather, it is a modality of pure familiarity. We will presently give a logic that captures both familiarity and epistemic modality in this sense.

8.5 Logical Omniscience

All normal systems of modal logic contain a rule of the form[29]

From $\vdash \varphi$ infer $\vdash \Box\varphi$.

where $\Box$ is a modal operator roughly similar to the S_i operators in our logic.

If the operator in question is understood epistemically, this leads to the so called logical omniscience problem, viz, each agent knows all logical truths. Even in our logic of familiarity, as long as we limit ourselves to meaningful terms, we can attribute arbitrarily complex logical truths to agents. Various attempts have been made to solve logical omniscience and related problems by restricting the logic in one way or another (cf. e.g., Eberle 1974; Fagin and Halpern 1988; Levesque 1985, 1990). Other research has been done on analyzing the complexity issues in reasoning about knowledge and belief (cf. e.g., Goldwasser et al. 1985, Halpern and Vardi 1986, Vardi 1989, Halpern and Moses 1992). Nonetheless, for some uses this kind of omniscience may be a reasonable assumption, hence not a problem at all. For example, in cryptographic protocol analysis, the area out of which the logic of chapter 7 first developed, one is concerned with the ability of some hostile agent to subvert a protocol in some way. While it may be unrealistic to attribute knowledge of all logical truths to such an agent, it may simplify analysis greatly to assume that the agent has such knowledge. By doing so we may conclude that he can obtain knowledge via certain protocols that he

---

[29]In alethic logics this rule is usually called Necessitation. For an explication of 'normal' cf. Chellas 1980, pp. 113–ff.

actually cannot, but doing so will never lead us to conclude that he cannot obtain knowledge that he can. And, the gain in ease of analysis may offset the unrealistic nature of the assumption.

While perhaps useful in some contexts, epistemic generalization is too strong a rule for any general representation of knowledge. (Even in the context cited above, it might be handy to limit the rule to knowledge operators corresponding to hostile agents rather than allowing it for all knowledge operators.) Positing the ideal rationality implicit in such a rule as epistemic generalization seems patently unrealistic. Not only does knowledge of logical truths vary from individual to individual but also from situation to situation for the same individual. Therefore, it seems far more reasonable to simply abandon such an idealization and to set out our assumptions about the known formulae in specific situations just as we set out the known individual terms in specific situations. One way to pursue this line would be to limit awareness at a world to some subset of the primitive propositions. In a sense we have already done this: any formula containing an undefined term is itself undefined. But, this does not preclude unrealistic knowledge of very complicated formulae. For, we can still construct arbitrarily large formulae out of the known ones. This could be avoided by restricting logical closure in some way so that even though, e.g., an agent is aware of φ and ψ in a situation, he is not aware of $\varphi \wedge \psi$ in that situation. This is a feature of the approach taken by Fagin and Halpern (1988), and of the approach taken in the next chapter.

8.6 Epistemic Situations

Recall that our situations are meant to capture different possible conceptions of the world. Any knower, any cognitive agent, might potentially know infinitely many things. But, any knower that we are interested in representing, be it a person or a computer process or whatever, knows only finitely many things in any given situation. And, our basic world structure should reflect this. Trying to reflect this while remaining as close as we can to traditional possible worlds might lead us to determine a world by the (finite) set of formulae that are true there. But, we need something more. A conceptual world should reflect not only what is true (and false) but also what is understood. For instance, while I might believe that it is raining outside my window right now, I understand the statement that it is not raining outside my window right now. This understanding is not determined by the truth values I attach to statements (except for some special cases to be discussed below). Truth values, however, are affected by understanding since, in a conceptual world, a formula cannot be true or false if it is not understood.

This is not quite as trivial as it would be for alethic worlds. Because of the limited cognitive nature of our worlds, without imposing some constraints, the true formulae would not necessarily determine the false formulae and the domain of quantification. We now give constraints to determine these.

The domain appears to be easily handled; we simply require that if $a(t) \in d(w)$ then $t = t \in w$. This conditions seems to be consistent with the cognitive nature of our situations. It requires only that self-identity statements be understood for terms understood in a situation. (Note: it does not even require that identity statements between understood terms be understood at a world but merely that *self*-identity statements involving understood terms be understood.) Admittedly one could conceive of a cognitive agent for which this condition failed to hold; however, unlike the typical idealizations that occur in epistemic logics, this seems to be very trivial. It is hard to imagine what of significance is lost by assuming it.

Unfortunately, self-identity statements are not as innocuous as they seem. In the last chapter, we did not distinguish the names under which an individual was known in determining that the individual was known. Thus, assuming names for the natural numbers and the standard arithmetic functions are acceptable term building parts of our language, '2' denotes at a world if and only if '$9116 - 294 \times (3 + 17 + 11)$' denotes there. This may make sense when we are primarily concerned with familiarity. In the context of awareness, it is not clear that we want $9116 - 294 \times (3 + 17 + 11) = 9116 - 294 \times (3 + 17 + 11) \in w$ whenever $2 = 2 \in w$. Note that we are not even broaching whether $9116 - 294 \times (3 + 17 + 11) = 2 \in w$. The point is that if two is in $d(w)$, then on this proposal, any self-identity for a term that denotes two is in w, no matter how complex.

Still the difficulty may be elsewhere than with our proposed requirement. Even in epistemic contexts, "No entity without identity," seems a good maxim to live by. The requirement may just be highlighting a problem with our determination of domains in the context of awareness. In fact a solution may be to add the converse of the proposed requirement. In other words $a(t) \in d(w)$ if $t = t \in w$. We will return to this discussion after we have set out our semantics of awareness in the next chapter.

Capturing the false formulae also seems tricky. We could require that $\neg \varphi \in w$ for any φ that is false at w. But, under our current assignment function, if φ were false at w this would imply the presence in w of all formulae with an odd number of negation symbols in front of φ, which hardly makes w finite. Instead we essentially require that if a formula φ is assigned F at w, then $\neg\varphi \in w$. In other words, that $\neg\varphi \in w$ is a necessary but not sufficient condition for φ to be assigned F at w. This condition only requires that if a formula is understood to be false, then its negation is understood. Here too it is hard to imagine what of significance is lost by assuming it. (In fact, given the understanding of negation and truth value assignments to be set out in the next chapter, it is hard to imagine how a cognitive agent could fail to satisfy this condition.)

In our discussion so far we have been speaking as if a world is not only determined by the set of formulae true there, it is also constituted of those formulae. There is an alternative. We could continue to treat worlds atomically as we had previously. In this sense they would serve essentially as indices to determine the terms and formulae that are understood at the given world. Thus, in the definition of a model we would need a function h to determine the understood formulae in addition to the function d, which determines domains. This is somewhat like the approach taken by Fagin and Halpern (1988) except that their awareness function is indexed to both worlds and individuals. In their semantics different individuals can be aware of different formulae in the same situation. Once we have done this, we have lost the intuitive semantic motivation that we started with, that of having worlds that are themselves epistemically rather than metaphysically based. The semantics of awareness to be given presently retains this motivation.

9

A Logic of Awareness

> When I considered a concept or a proposition occurring in a scientific or philosophical discussion, I thought that I understood it clearly only if I felt that I could express it, if I wanted to, in a symbolic language.
> —Rudolf Carnap in his "Intellectual Autobiography"

The language and logic that we set out in chapter 7 is adequate to represent knowledge of individuals in the sense of familiarity. A goal of this chapter is to give a logic and language adequate for the syntactic characterization of the shared situation account of common knowledge set out in chapter 4. We have already explored this area to some extent by looking at expansions and revisions of the logic of familiarity. In this chapter we will look at another logic that shares some of the features of that one but does not have the problems mentioned at the end of section 8.2.

9.1 A Semantics of Awareness

Our object language is the same as in the language of familiarity except for the following modifications. Amongst the individual constant symbols: $a, b, c, \ldots$ we distinguish a set of situation constants referring to situations (possible worlds): $w_1, w_2, w_3, \ldots$ These may stand in all the places where ordinary constants go. We also distinguish amongst the individual variables a set of variables that can only be instantiated with situation constants: $z_1, z_2, z_3, \ldots$. We also add '$\models$' to the object language as follows. If 'w' is a situation constant and 'φ' is any formula, then '$w \models \varphi$' is a formula. (Note that we do not yet add formulae to represent knowing situations as we discussed in section 8.2. Later in this chapter we will discuss how to define these.)

9.2 Models

A model is a tuple $\langle D, W, R_1, \ldots R_n, h, \iota, \{\iota_w\}_{w \in W}, a \rangle$ where W is a set of nonempty possible worlds; R_1, ..., R_n are reflexive binary accessibility relations between members of W; and D is a domain of objects for all possible worlds. Since worlds themselves are objects, $W \subseteq D$.

The function h goes from members of W to finite sets of formulae in the language; it gives the terms and formulae understood in different situations. We require that understood equations be composed only of understood terms. Thus, $f(t_1, \ldots, t_k) = t \in h(w)$ only if $(t_1 = t_1), \ldots, (t_k = t_k) \in h(w)$, and $(t = t) \in h(w)$. Similarly, understood formulae should be composed of understood formulae containing understood terms. Thus, $\varphi \in h(w)$ only if all hereditary subformulae of φ are in $h(w)$ and $t = t \in h(w)$ for any constant term t occurring in φ. Note that we represent that a term t is understood at a world by having $t = t \in h(w)$. Finally, we require that h be closed under the general properties of equality. In other words, we require the following: $s = t \in h(w)$ and $\varphi \in h(w)$ imply $\varphi' \in h(w)$ and $\varphi'' \in h(w)$ (where φ' is the result of replacing some or all occurrences of t in φ with s, and φ'' is the result of replacing some or all occurrences of s in φ with t). These restrictions amount to our minimal closure conditions on rational awareness.

The function ι is a one-one function from terms in the language to members of the domain. Note that this means that every distinct name denotes a distinct object. It might seem that this would preclude one's knowing, for example, that Mark Twain is Samuel Clemens. That is not the case. It will become clear below that, in w, Robbie knows that Mark Twain is Samuel Clemens precisely when these names pick out the same thing at all worlds accessible from w for him. What ι being one-one allows us to express in our framework is the possibility that Robbie does not know that Mark Twain is Samuel Clemens. Recall that we have constant terms for denoting worlds in our language. The family of functions $\{\iota_w\}_{w \in W}$ determines the denotation of terms at each world. $\iota_w(t)$ is a set of individuals $\iota(s)$ such that $s = t \in h(w)$. In particular, ι_w partitions the set $\{\iota(s) : s = s \in h(w)\}$. This guarantees that all and only understood terms denote in our (epistemic) worlds. So, each ι_w gives rise to an equivalence relation on terms that determines which terms denote the same individuals at each world. Continuing our example from above, at all worlds w' accessible for Robbie from w, $\iota_{w'}$('Samuel Clemens') = $\iota_{w'}$('Mark Twain') = an equivalence class containing both ι('Samuel Clemens') and ι('Mark Twain'). Note that an individual in a world is a set of individuals in D: individuals in D are distinguished in the language but might not be in a particular world. If $t = t \notin h(w)$, then $\iota_w(t) = \emptyset$, which we understand as saying that t denotes nothing at that world. While technically t is assigned $\emptyset$ at w rather than nothing, with respect to terms '$\emptyset$' in this chapter is playing the same role as '$*$' did in chapter 7. Each ι_w assigns values to tuples of terms such that $\iota_w(\langle t_1, \ldots, t_n \rangle) = \langle \iota_w(t_1), \ldots, \iota_w(t_n) \rangle$. Each ι_w also assigns a value to each predicate constant in the language. For an n-ary predicate constant P, $\iota_w(P) = \{\iota_w(\langle t_{1_1}, \ldots, t_{1_n} \rangle), \ldots, \iota_w(\langle t_{k_1}, \ldots, t_{k_n} \rangle)\}$, where $\iota_w(t_{j_m}) \neq \emptyset$. Note that while no member of a tuple in $\iota_w(P)$ may be nondenoting, it is possible that $\iota_w(P) = \emptyset$, in other words that P is nondenoting at w. ('Nondenoting' is understood for predicate constants in the same sense that it is understood for terms.) There will be a further restriction on the ι_w determined by the assignment function, which we will introduce at the appropriate place.

The function a assigns truth values to formulae in our language in the manner given below. As in chapter 7 we want to allow a to be undefined sometimes; thus we again use the standard trick of adding a value '$*$' to represent being undefined. Unlike its usage in chapter 7, a only assigns truth values. It does not assign values to terms or predicate letters. Also unlike chapter 7, a is entirely relative. That is, a only takes values at situations and thus is a function of two arguments, a situation and a formula. For convenience we generally write things in terms of the naturally induced family of situation projection functions associated with a. In other words, $a(w, \varphi) = a_w(\varphi)$ for all $w \in W$ and φ in the language.

We make one more constraint on rational awareness that relates h and a. Specifically, we want to require that any understood formula receives a determinate truth value. It might seem that a sentence can be understood without a decision as to its truth value. I might understand the claim that the president is in Washington right now without knowing whether it is true or false. But, this is really only a reflection of our limited terminology. The understanding in this case is that of an individual not that of a situation. To say that I understand the claim but don't know whether it is true or false is to say that I accept as possible both a situation where it is true and one where it is false. But, each of these situations does attach a determinate truth value to the claim. Saying that formulae in the image of $h(w)$ are understood at w may thus be a little deceptive. Nothing in the individual cases for types of formulae below forces or precludes this constraint. Therefore, we stipulate up front that $\varphi \in h(w)$ implies either $a_w(\varphi) = \text{T}$ or $a_w(\varphi) = \text{F}$. (Note that the cases for formula types will imply that in the latter case $\neg\varphi \in h(w)$ as well.)

The Assignment Function

The a_w assign truth values to formulae as follows:

$$a_w(s = t) = \begin{cases} \text{T} & \text{if } s = t \in h(w) \text{ and } \iota_w(s) = \iota_w(t) \\ \text{F} & \text{if } s \neq t \in h(w) \text{ and } \iota_w(s) \neq \iota_w(t) \\ * & \text{otherwise} \end{cases}$$

$$a_w(C_i(t)) = \begin{cases} \text{T} & \text{if } \iota_{w'}(t) \neq \emptyset \text{ for all } w' \text{ s.t. } wR_iw' \text{ }^{30} \\ \text{F} & \text{if } \iota_w(t) \neq \emptyset \text{ and } \iota_{w'}(t) = \emptyset \text{ for some } w' \text{ s.t. } wR_iw' \\ * & \text{otherwise} \end{cases}$$

For k-ary predicate letters P, other than equality and C_i (for $i = 1, \ldots, n$), we have

$$a_w(P(t_1, \ldots, t_k)) = \begin{cases} \text{T} & \text{if } \iota_w(\langle t_1, \ldots, t_k \rangle) \in \iota_w(P) \text{ and} \\ & P(t_1, \ldots, t_k) \in h(w) \\ \text{F} & \text{if } \iota_w(\langle t_1, \ldots, t_k \rangle) \notin \iota_w(P) \text{ and} \\ & \neg P(t_1, \ldots, t_k) \in h(w) \\ * & \text{otherwise} \end{cases}$$

For an arbitrary sentence φ,

$$a_w(S_i\varphi) = \begin{cases} \text{T} & \text{if } S_i\varphi \in h(w) \text{ and} \\ & a_{w'}(\varphi) = \text{T, for all } w' \text{ s.t. } wR_iw' \\ \text{F} & \text{if } \neg(S_i\varphi) \in h(w), \text{ and} \\ & a_{w'}(\varphi) \text{ is defined for all } w' \text{ s.t. } wR_iw', \\ & \text{and } a_{w'}(\varphi) = \text{F for some } w' \text{ s.t. } wR_iw' \\ * & \text{otherwise} \end{cases}$$

$$a_w(\forall x\varphi) = \begin{cases} \text{T} & \text{if } \forall x\varphi \in h(w) \text{ and} \\ & a_w(\varphi[t/x]) = \text{T, for all } t \text{ s.t. } \iota_w(t) \neq \emptyset \\ \text{F} & \text{if } \neg\forall x\varphi \in h(w) \text{ and} \\ & a_w(\varphi[t/x]) = \text{F, for some } t \text{ s.t. } \iota_w(t) \neq \emptyset \\ * & \text{otherwise} \end{cases}$$

where $\varphi[t/x]$ is the same sentence as φ except that all free occurrences of x in φ are replaced by t

---

[30] Recall that $\iota_{w'}(t) \neq \emptyset$ implies $t = t \in h(w')$.

$$a_w(\varphi \wedge \psi) = \begin{cases} T & \text{if } (\varphi \wedge \psi) \in h(w) \text{ and} \\ & a_w(\varphi) = T \text{ and } a_w(\psi) = T \\ F & \text{if } \neg(\varphi \wedge \psi) \in h(w) \text{ and} \\ & a_w(\varphi) = F \text{ or } a_w(\psi) = F \\ & \text{and both } a_w(\varphi) \text{ and } a_w(\psi) \text{ are defined} \\ * & \text{otherwise} \end{cases}$$

$$a_w(\varphi \vee \psi) = \begin{cases} T & \text{if } (\varphi \vee \psi) \in h(w) \text{ and} \\ & a_w(\varphi) = T \text{ or } a_w(\psi) = T \\ & \text{and both } a_w(\varphi) \text{ and } a_w(\psi) \text{ are defined} \\ F & \text{if } \neg(\varphi \vee \psi) \in h(w) \text{ and} \\ & a_w(\varphi) = F \text{ and } a_w(\psi) = F \\ * & \text{otherwise} \end{cases}$$

$$a_w(\varphi \to \psi) = \begin{cases} T & \text{if } (\varphi \to \psi) \in h(w) \text{ and} \\ & a_w(\varphi) = F \text{ or } a_w(\psi) = T \\ & \text{and both } a_w(\varphi) \text{ and } a_w(\psi) \text{ are defined} \\ F & \text{if } \neg(\varphi \to \psi) \in h(w) \text{ and} \\ & a_w(\varphi) = T \text{ and } a_w(\psi) = F \\ * & \text{otherwise} \end{cases}$$

$$a_w(\neg\varphi) = \begin{cases} T & \text{if } \neg\varphi \in h(w) \text{ and } a_w(\varphi) = F \\ F & \text{if } \neg\neg\varphi \in h(w) \text{ and } a_w(\varphi) = T \\ * & \text{otherwise} \end{cases}$$

The assignment function for formulae of the form $w \models \varphi$ can now be properly expressed using the h function and the ι function as,

$$a_w(w' \models \varphi) = \begin{cases} T & \text{if } \iota_w(w') \neq \emptyset, (w'' \models \varphi) \in h(w), \text{ and} \\ & a_{w''}(\varphi) = T \text{ for all } w'' \in \iota_w(w') \\ F & \text{if } \iota_w(w') \neq \emptyset, \neg(w'' \models \varphi) \in h(w), \text{ and} \\ & \text{either } a_{w''}(\varphi) = F \text{ or } a_{w''}(\varphi) = * \\ & \text{for all } w'' \in \iota_w(w') \\ * & \text{otherwise} \end{cases}$$

Domains

Given our emphasis on world relative domains in this and the last two chapters it may be surprising that our models do not have the d function of the models for familiarity, which determined the domain at each world. We have not given up world relative domains; rather, the interpretation ι_w determines the domain of w. The domain of a world w is simply $\{\iota_w(t) : \iota_w(t) \neq \emptyset\}$. We have no need of a special domain function, but for convenience in the context of this discussion, we let $d(w) = \{\iota_w(t) : \iota_w(t) \neq \emptyset\}$.

What is the relationship between the understood terms of w, $\{t : t = t \in h(w)\}$ and the terms in the domain of w? Under the constraints set out above, $(t = t) \in h(w)$ if and only if $\iota_w(t) \in d(w)$. But, this need not be the case. We could constrain h and d such that $t = t \in h(w)$ only if $\iota_w(t) \in d(w)$ while allowing that the converse may fail to hold. Then $\iota_w(t)$ might be understood in a situation without being understood *qua* the denotatum of 't'. This would allow us to naturally distinguish between, e.g., Eleri knowing Jenna as the person named by 'Jenna' and Eleri simply knowing Jenna. (This could be a distinction with a difference since, at the time of first writing, both Eleri and Jenna were in the neighborhood of two years old.) The first of these would be represented in our language by '$S_e(j = j)$', where syntactic expressions are connected to the obvious people. The second of these would be represented in our language by $C_e j$. No doubt it is useful for making some distinctions to have these two notions of an individual being understood at a world; however, to have a term denote at a world without itself being understood there is antithetical to the epistemic nature we expect our worlds to have.

Perhaps the opposite is what we need: we could constrain h and d such that $\iota_w(t) \in d(w)$ only if $(t = t) \in h(w)$ while allowing that the converse of this may fail to hold. This would allow us to distinguish t being comprehensible from t existing. Thus, 'Sherlock Holmes is a famous Victorian sleuth.' may be understandable and even true despite the fact that Holmes does not exist. This is not antithetical to the epistemic nature of our worlds. We can have 's' be understood and fail to denote (an existing thing). In this case, that 's' fails to denote is understood. Assuming 's' names Sherlock Holmes, we could capture this state of affairs, w, by having $s = s \in h(w)$, but $\iota_w(s) \notin d(w)$. Thus, all the usual claims about Holmes would be true: that he's a famous sleuth, that Dr. Watson is his assistant, etc. Nonetheless, he does not exist at w. While the ability to make the distinction is desirable, this would not be the appropriate way to make it in our framework. To adopt this approach would be to use domains (and quantification) to handle fictional objects in a manner similar free logic. But, as discussed in section 7.2, our domains determine the meaningful and the understood rather than the existent. This is as true for the current logic as for the logic of familiarity.

Given that our interests and our use of domains are entirely different from those of free logics, handling existence in the sense that distinguishes the fictional from the real is trivial for us. We can simply introduce an ordinary unary predicate letter, say 'E', to pick out those things that exist from those things that don't. For us 'E' is not tied in any way to existential quantification.

9.3 Axioms and Rules

In contrast to our presentation of the logic of familiarity we do not attempt to make all axioms true at all worlds. We therefore do not restrict axioms to formulae not containing any (free) constant terms. We will of course require that axioms not be false. Thus, they will be true whenever they are defined.

Axioms are the universal closures of the following.

1. $\varphi \rightarrow (\psi \rightarrow \varphi)$
2. $(\varphi \rightarrow (\psi \rightarrow \gamma)) \rightarrow ((\varphi \rightarrow \psi) \rightarrow (\varphi \rightarrow \gamma))$
3. $(\neg\psi \rightarrow \neg\varphi) \rightarrow (\neg\psi \rightarrow (\varphi \rightarrow \psi))$
4. $S_i(\varphi) \wedge S_i(\varphi \rightarrow \psi) \rightarrow S_i(\psi)$
5. $S_i(\varphi) \rightarrow \varphi$
6. $\forall x(x = x)$
7. $\forall x \forall y((x = y) \rightarrow (\varphi \rightarrow \varphi'))$
    (where φ' is the result of replacing no, some or all occurrences of 'x' in φ with 'y')
8. $S_i\varphi \rightarrow C_i t$
    (where φ is an arbitrary sentence and t is any term occurring freely in φ)
9. $(w \models (\varphi \wedge \psi)) \rightarrow ((w \models \varphi) \wedge (w \models \psi))$
10. $(w \models (\varphi \vee \psi)) \rightarrow ((w \models \varphi) \vee (w \models \psi))$
11. $(w \models \neg\varphi) \rightarrow \neg(w \models \varphi)$
12. $(w \models \varphi) \rightarrow ((w \models \psi) \vee (w \models \neg\psi))$
    (where ψ is any hereditary subformula of φ)
13. $(w \models (\varphi \rightarrow \psi)) \rightarrow (w \models \varphi) \rightarrow (w \models \psi)$
14. $(w \models \varphi) \rightarrow (w \models (t = t))$
    (where φ is an arbitrary sentence and t is any term occurring freely in φ)
15. $(w \models S_i\varphi) \rightarrow (w \models \varphi)$
16. $((w \models S_i\varphi) \wedge (w \models S_i(\varphi \rightarrow \psi))) \rightarrow (w \models S_i\psi)$
17. $(w \models \forall x\varphi) \rightarrow (w \models t = t) \rightarrow (w \models \varphi[t/x])$
18. $(w \models C_i t) \rightarrow (w \models S_i \forall x\varphi) \rightarrow (w \models S_i\varphi[t/x])$
19. $(w \models v \models \varphi) \rightarrow (v \models \varphi)$
20. $(w \models \varphi) \rightarrow (w \models \psi)$
    (where ψ is any axiom that is a hereditary subformula of φ)

21. $(w \models \varphi) \to \psi$
   (where ψ is any axiom that is a hereditary subformula of φ)
22. $(w \models \psi \to (Mt \to \varphi)) \land ((w \models \forall x \varphi[x/t]) \lor (w \models \neg \forall x \varphi[x/t])) \to (w \models \psi \to \forall x \varphi[x/t])$
   (where t is any term that does not occur freely in ψ)

Note that the Knowledge Relation rule of chapter 7 has been replaced by an axiom. This is permissible because we loosened the requirement that all axioms be true. Most of the other new axioms are present to insure that logical behavior of the satisfaction relation respects standard intuitions. The one that may seem least intuitive is axiom 19. Roughly, it says that if a situation w says that φ is true in another situation v, then φ is true in v. It might seem that this is too high a price to pay for expressibility. Why should what is true in one world force what is true in another?

There are a few ways of looking at the answer to this. First, recall that our worlds are epistemic. Epistemic logics ordinarily interpret epistemic modality in a world structure that is derived from motivations of alethic modal logic. Thus, the worlds are simply 'out there' to be differentiated or not by knowers. In other words knowledge is imposed from the top down, based on how finely the knower is able to separate into groups all the possible worlds. Nonetheless, even the ordinary approach to epistemic modality enforces some restriction on how the worlds are constructed. (In other words, the bottom up view.) If $S_i \varphi$ is true at a given world w, then it is impossible for w to also make true $S_j \neg \varphi$ for any j. Of course this is just a consistency constraint forced on us by axiom 5. Axiom 19 simply forces another consistency. The problem is that the constraint it enforces seems to lack the intuitive motivation of that imposed by axiom 5.

In more ordinary approaches to possible world semantics, there is nothing epistemic about the worlds themselves. This is not just a comment about the absence of cognitive or computability limitations (the 'out there' feature just mentioned). Epistemic logics are semantically distinguished from doxastic logics by the accessibility relations. In our more bottom up approach, given our ability to talk about situations themselves, the differentiation between epistemic and doxastic logic appears not just in the accessibility relations but also in the situations. If in w it is true that $v \models \varphi$, then this is something about which w cannot be mistaken.

Put another way, this axiom simply insures that we don't use the same name to refer to distinct situations u and v in distinct situations w and w'. We don't account for the possibility that two situations mistakenly refer to different situations as the same. Situations are referred to in both the object language and the metalanguage. Thus, they must respect the metalinguistic truths of some theoretical perspective. And, it is not possible to consistently respect two conflicting perspectives for the naming of situations.

The logical rules are as follows:

R1. (Modus Ponens) From φ and $\varphi \to \psi$ infer ψ.

R2. (Universal Instantiation) From $\forall x \varphi \land Mt$ infer $\varphi[t/x]$.

(for any term t, where φ is a sentence in the language, and $\varphi[t/x]$ is the same sentence as φ except that all free occurrences of x in φ are replaced by t)

R3. (Universal Generalization) From $\psi \to (Mt \to \varphi)$ and $\forall x \varphi[x/t] \lor \neg \forall x \varphi[x/t]$ infer $\psi \to \forall x \varphi[x/t]$.

(where t is any term that does not occur freely in ψ or in any assumption on which $\psi \to (Mt \to \varphi)$ depends)

Except Universal Generalization, these rules are the same as in chapter 7. Universal Generalization has been changed simply to account for awareness of the universally quantified formula. We have already discussed those from the logic of familiarity that have been eliminated.

9.4 Metalogic

Soundness

Our soundness theorem is slightly different from the usual one because it is possible for axioms to fail to be true in a situation when they are not understood there. (But, they cannot be false in any situation.) Therefore, it is possible to derive a result using formulae that are not understood at a world, hence not true, and thus to arrive at a conclusion that is also not understood at that world.

We could have kept the usual form for the soundness theorem by modifying the understanding of '⊢' slightly. Ordinarily '$\Gamma \vdash \varphi$' is understood to mean that φ follows via the logical rules from Γ *and* the axioms. In other words, every line of a derivation is either a member of Γ, an axiom, or follows from previous lines by application of a rule. On the alternative reading of '⊢', any axioms used in a derivation must be explicitly included in Γ when we claim that $\Gamma \vdash \varphi$ (for any formula φ). The decision about which way to use '⊢' is largely a philosophical one depending on whether we want to emphasize epistemic concerns in our notation for derivability. There is a technical decision as well, but on a level of convenience rather than on an absolute level. If we retain the usual understanding of '⊢', we get a soundness theorem that is of a slightly nonstandard form. But, it also makes for a slightly less awkward completeness proof. We will opt for the more standard usage. This should also make for less confusion on the part of the reader.

To deal with the weakening of semantic constraints on axioms we introduce the following terminology. A formula φ is *weakly valid* in a model iff for all worlds in that model, $\varphi \in h(w)$ implies $a_w(\varphi) = \text{T}$. Also, throughout this chapter it is assumed that we are dealing only with finite sets of formulae. (Thus, compactness is simply a non-issue.) Syntactic derivation is generally taken as a finite phenomenon. But, given the cognitive nature of our situations, it is only natural to view semantic consequence as finite also.

Theorem 13 (Soundness) *If $\Gamma \vdash \varphi$ and $\varphi \in h(w)$ for all worlds w such that $\Gamma \subseteq h(w)$, then $\Gamma \models \varphi$.*

Proof. Despite the unorthodox nature of our logic, this proof is still fairly standard. As usual, we need the following lemma.

Lemma 14 *All axioms are weakly valid in all models.*

Proof. This result follows directly by inspection of the assignment function. □

We now proceed to prove the theorem by showing that all the ways that φ can follow from Γ are ways that preserve truth.

φ is a member of Γ. Then $\Gamma \models \varphi$ trivially.

φ is obtained by modus ponens from ψ and $\psi \to \varphi$. We first show that, for any world w, φ is in $h(w)$ provided that all members of Γ are in $h(w)$. We proceed via strong induction. Let w be any situation such that all members of Γ are in $h(w)$. Suppose that formulae on all previous lines of the derivation are in $h(w)$. Then, by assumption, $(\psi \to \varphi) \in h(w)$. So, $\varphi \in h(w)$ by closure of h under hereditary subformulae. Once this is shown, the rest of the argument is *verbatim* the one in chapter 7. (Viz, the result follows by a trivial argument via strong induction and by the definition of the assignment function. Suppose that soundness holds for all lines of a derivation up to the one in question, where φ occurs. Then, by inductive hypothesis, $\Gamma \models \psi$ and $\Gamma \models \psi \to \varphi$. So, clearly $\Gamma \models \varphi$ by the definition of the assignment function.)

φ is obtained by universal instantiation. Then φ is of the form $\psi[t/x]$. Proceeding by induction, we assume $\Gamma \models \forall x \psi \wedge Mt$. So, $\Gamma \models \forall x \psi$ and $\Gamma \models Mt$. If x does not occur freely in ψ, then $\forall x \psi$ is true iff ψ is true, and ψ is $\psi[t/x]$ in this case. So $\Gamma \models \psi[t/x]$. If x does occur freely in ψ, then $\Gamma \models \psi[t/x]$ by the definition of the assignment function.

φ **is obtained by universal generalization.** So, φ is of the form $\psi \to \forall x\theta[x/t]$, and, by inductive hypothesis, $\Gamma \,|\!\models \psi \to Mt \to \theta$ where t is an arbitrary term not occurring freely in ψ or any member of Γ. We may assume $\Gamma \,|\!\models \psi$. (If ψ is false, the result is trivial—since the second premise of the rule guarantees that $\forall x\theta[x/t]$ has a determinate truth value. And, if ψ is undefined, by inductive hypothesis, all of Γ is undefined and again the result is trivial.) So, by definition of the assignment function, $\Gamma \,|\!\models \psi \to \forall x\theta[x/t]$.

□

Completeness

Our completeness result is the same as in chapter 7; however, the details of the proof are substantially different.

Theorem 15 (Completeness) *If* $\Gamma \,|\!\models \varphi$, *then* $\Gamma \vdash \varphi$.

Proof. We again give a Henkin style proof for the completeness of the logic. But, unlike the typical procedure for such proofs, we cannot use maximality of consistent sets of sentences since all our worlds satisfy at most finitely many formulae. This means that our construction of the canonical model cannot proceed via Lindenbauming; nonetheless, the basic proof strategy remains the same. We construct a model where the worlds are (finite) consistent sets of sentences that are maximal in a sense to be spelled out presently, and that are subject to certain conditions. We then show that every such set is satisfiable.

Definition 1 Given a (consistent) set of formulae Γ, a set of formulae w is *maximal consistent with respect to* Γ if

- w is consistent,
- for every φ that is a hereditary subformula of a member of Γ, either φ or $\neg\varphi$ is in w, and
- if $s = t \in \Gamma$ and $\varphi \in \Gamma$, then all formulae φ' that are the result of replacing some or all occurrences of s in φ with t or the result of replacing some or all of the occurrences of t in φ with s are in w.

We now proceed to the construction of the canonical model. Let Γ be a finite consistent set of formulae of our language. We construct a set Γ' from Γ in two steps. First, if $s = t \in \Gamma$ and $\varphi \in \Gamma$, then add to Γ all formulae φ' that are the result of replacing some or all occurrences of s in φ with t or the result of replacing some or all of the occurrences of t in φ with s. Then add $S_i(t = t)$ to the resulting set for all t (and i) such that $C_i(t)$ is in the set that results from the first stage of construction.

In order to construct all sets of formulae that contain Γ' and are maximally consistent with respect to it, we order the hereditary subformulae of members of Γ'. Recall the characterization of complexity of formulae.

1. Any atomic formula has complexity 1.
2. Given two formulae φ and ψ, and of complexity m and n respectively.
   - The complexity of $\forall x \varphi$ is $m + 1$.
   - The complexity of $\neg \varphi$ is $m + 1$.
   - The complexity of $\varphi \wedge \psi$ is $\max\{m, n\} + 1$.
   - The complexity of $\varphi \vee \psi$ is $\max\{m, n\} + 1$.
3. To the usual characterization we simply add that given a formula φ of complexity m and given a world term w, the complexity of $w \models \varphi$ is $m + 1$.

We now construct an ordering on the hereditary subformulae of Γ' as follows:

1. List the atomic hereditary subformulae of Γ' in any order.
2. List all formulae not containing any occurrences of the satisfaction symbol '$\models$' in order of increasing complexity. (List formulae of the same complexity in any order.)
3. List all formulae of the form $w \models \varphi$ according to the order that φ appeared previously in the list (including φ of the form $v \models \psi$).
4. List all boolean combinations and quantifications over previous formulae in the list in increasing order of complexity.
5. Repeat steps 3 and 4 until all the hereditary subformulae of Γ' have been listed.

This procedure will produce a finite list of formulae, $\{\varphi_1, \ldots, \varphi_n\}$. We next use this list to construct our situations. Let $w_1, \ldots, w_m$ be all the world terms occurring in Γ (hence in Γ'). Make m lists of the formulae in Γ' and label them $w_1, \ldots, w_m$ respectively. (If there are no world terms in Γ, make one list labeled w.) We next add the subformulae by proceeding along the list we produced and adding (in order) each formula or its negation to all the worlds according to the following criteria.

- If φ is consistent with the already present members of $w_{j,\ldots}$ and $\neg\varphi$ is not, add φ to $w_{j,\ldots}$. (The ellipsis will be explained presently.)
- If $\neg\varphi$ is consistent with the already present members of $w_{j,\ldots}$ and φ is not, add $\neg\varphi$ to $w_{j,\ldots}$.

- If φ and $\neg\varphi$ are both consistent with the already present members of $w_{j,\ldots}$, split the list into $w_{j,\ldots,0}$ containing φ and $w_{j,\ldots,1}$ containing $\neg\varphi$.
- After each formula is added to a world, close that world under the conditions that took us from Γ to Γ' before proceeding.

We have now constructed all sets of formulae that are maximal consistent with respect to Γ'; however, the presence of formulae involving the satisfaction relation requires us to do more before we have a set of situations to serve as W in our canonical model. First, our construction may have rendered all such formulae undefined since there may no longer be situations named by the world terms with which we started. We can solve this by choosing for each world w_j mentioned in Γ any situation $w_{j,\ldots}$ to be the world named by w_j. Second, while each world is itself consistent we need to be sure that the set of worlds that constitute W is *situation consistent* as a whole. That is, for a formula of the form $w_j \models \psi$ to be in a world w we must make sure that this is consistent with w and also that ψ is in w_j. Since Γ is itself consistent it must be possible to choose worlds $w_1, \ldots, w_m$ from amongst the $w_{1,\ldots}, \ldots, w_{m,\ldots}$ respectively so that the resulting collection of sets of formulae is situation consistent. This set is W.

We are now in a position to present the canonical model, $\langle D, W, R_1, \ldots R_n, h, \iota, \{\iota_w\}_{w \in W}, a \rangle$.

- $D = \{t : t \text{ is a term of the language}\}$,
- W is as set out above,
- $R_i = \{\langle w, w' \rangle : S_i\varphi \in w \Rightarrow \varphi \in w'\}$ for all i in $\{1, \ldots, n\}$,
- $h(w) = \{\varphi : \varphi \text{ is either } \psi \text{ or } \neg\psi \text{ and } \psi \in w\}$ for all $w \in W$,
- $\iota(t) = t$ for all constant terms t in the language,
- $\iota_w(t) = \{s : s = t \text{ or } t = s \in w\}$ for all constant terms t in the language and $w \in W$,
- $\iota_w(P) = \{\langle t_1, \ldots, t_k \rangle : P(t_1, \ldots, t_k) \in w\}$ for any (k-ary) predicate constant P,
- a is as set out in section 9.2.

With the specification of the canonical model finished we proceed to the main step in our completeness proof, the truth lemma.

Lemma 16 *If φ is a formula of our language, then $a_w(\varphi) = T$ iff $\varphi \in w$.*

Proof. The proof proceeds by cases, all of which are either immediate or follow by trivial induction arguments.

116 / LOGIC, CONVENTION, AND COMMON KNOWLEDGE

Case i: (φ **is of the form** $\psi \wedge \theta$, $\psi \vee \theta$, $\psi \rightarrow \theta$, **or** $\neg\psi$) All of these follow by trivial inductive arguments. We present the case where φ is $\psi \vee \theta$ as an example. $a_w(\psi \vee \theta) = $ T iff $(\psi \vee \theta) \in h(w)$ and either $a_w(\psi) = $ T or $a_w(\theta) = $ T. By inductive hypothesis, this is true iff $(\psi \vee \theta) \in h(w)$ and either $\psi \in w$ or $\theta \in w$. And, by the definition of h and the consistency of w, this is so iff $(\psi \vee \theta) \in w$.

Case ii: (φ **is of the form** $s = t$) $s = t \in w$ iff $s = t \in h(w)$ and $\iota_w(s) = \iota_w(t)$ iff $a_w(s = t) = $ T.

Case iii: (φ **is of the form** $C_i t$) $C_i t \in w$ iff $C_i t \in h(w)$ and $S_i(t = t) \in w$ iff $\iota_{w'}(t) \neq \emptyset$ for all w' such that $wR_i w'$ iff $a_w(C_i t) = $ T.

Case iv: (φ **is of the form** $P(t_1, \ldots, t_k)$) $P(t_1, \ldots, t_k) \in w$ iff $P(t_1, \ldots, t_k) \in h(w)$ and $\iota_w(\langle t_1, \ldots, t_k \rangle) \in \iota_w(P)$ iff $a_w(P(t_1, \ldots, t_k)) = $ T.

Case v: (φ **is of the form** $S_i \psi$) $S_i \psi \in w$ iff $S_i(\psi) \in h(w)$ and $\psi \in w'$ for all w' such that $wR_i w'$, by definition of the canonical model. But, by inductive hypothesis, this is so iff $a_{w'}(\psi) = $ T for all such w' and $S_i(\psi) \in h(w)$, which is so iff $a_w(S_i \psi) = $ T.

Case vi: (φ **is of the form** $\forall x \psi$) By universal instantiation, maximal consistency, and the definition of h, $\forall x \psi \in w$ iff $\forall x \psi \in h(w)$ and $\psi[t/x] \in w$ for all t such that $\iota_w(t) \neq \emptyset$. But, by inductive hypothesis, this is so iff $a_w(\psi[t/x]) = $ T for all t such that $\iota_w(t) \neq \emptyset$. And, by the definition of a, this is true iff $a_w(\forall x \psi) = $ T.

Case vii: (φ **is of the form** $v \models \psi$) $a_w(v \models \psi) = $ T iff $(v \models \psi) \in h(w)$ and $\iota_w(v) \neq \emptyset$ and $a_{v'}(\psi) = $ T for all $v' \in \iota_w(v)$. But, by inductive hypothesis, this is so iff $(v \models \psi) \in h(w)$ and $\iota_w(v) \neq \emptyset$ and $\psi \in v'$ for all $v' \in \iota_w(v)$. Thus, by the maximal consistency and situation consistency of our world construction, and by the definition of $h(w)$ and ι_w, this is so iff $(v \models \psi) \in w$.

□

Now that we have established the truth lemma, completeness follows immediately since we have shown that Γ (an arbitrary consistent set of sentences) is satisfied by the canonical model.

□

9.5 Adding Knowledge of Situations

A major goal of this chapter was to introduce a logic that is adequate to express and reason about common knowledge. The astute reader will have noticed that the language set out above is not expressive enough to do the job. We have yet to introduce a means to represent knowing that a situation obtains. Actually, it is possible to represent such knowledge with an eliminable syntactic definition. If we represent that agent i knows that v is the situation by $S_i v$, then we can define this as follows:

$$S_i v \leftrightarrow \bigwedge_{\varphi \in h(v)} ((v \models \varphi) \rightarrow (S_i \varphi \land S_i(v \models \varphi)))$$

Since $h(v)$ is finite for all v and since the formulae on the right are all well formed, $S_i v$ can always be completely eliminated from any formula (or finite set of formulae) and replaced by the longer expression. The semantics for such formulae are thus determined by the above definition as follows.

$$a_w(S_i v) = \begin{cases} \text{T} & \text{if } S_i v \in h(w), \text{ and for all } \varphi \text{ such that } a_v(\varphi) = \text{T} \\ & a_w(S_i \varphi) = \text{T and } a_w(S_i(v \models \varphi)) = \text{T} \\ \text{F} & \text{if } \neg S_i v \in h(w), \text{ and for some } \varphi \text{ s.t. } a_v(\varphi) = \text{T}, \\ & a_w(S_i \varphi) = \text{F or } a_w(S_i(v \models \varphi)) = \text{F} \\ * & \text{otherwise} \end{cases}$$

Recall that we had a syntactic definition of common knowledge in the previous chapter, viz:

$$S_{ij}\varphi \leftrightarrow \exists w(S_i w \land S_j w \land w \models S_i w \land w \models S_j w \land w \models \varphi)$$

It may thus seem that with the definition of formulae of the form $S_i w$ in place we can claim to have a sound and complete logic that can represent common knowledge. But that is too hasty. If we only use these formulae as abbreviations, we do have a sound and complete logic that can represent knowledge of situations. Once we allow these formulae as proper formulae of the language we are in a position where truth assignments may be nonwellfounded. For determination of truth value depends on the truth values of all the formulae in a situation. If $S_i v \in h(v)$, then to determine if $S_i v$ is true at v we must first know if all the formulae true at v are known, including $S_i v$ itself.

The problem is that there are different partitions of $h(v)$ into true and false formulae (at v and possibly elsewhere) that will satisfy the definition of the assignment. The solution is to stipulate that we always choose the one that yields the largest set of true formulae.[31] This is not to say that there is a unique largest set any more than it would for wellfounded truth assignments. Given a formula $(\varphi \lor \psi) \land \neg(\varphi \land \psi)$ with no other relevant constraints on φ and ψ there are two possible assignments making as many formulae as possible true amongst the

---

[31] Our approach has many similarities to that taken by Barwise (1989a) when he gives his co-inductive characterization of satisfaction.

hereditary subformulae of $(\varphi \vee \psi) \wedge \neg(\varphi \wedge \psi)$. But even if we must assign truth values to $S_i v$ and $S_i w$ subject to the constraint $\neg(S_i v \wedge S_i w)$, it is still possible to consistently make both of them false or only one. Our understanding of the assignment function is to make formulae of the form $S_i v$ true when it is consistent with our other decisions to do so.

We can capture this via a slightly more complicated assignment function as follows.

$$a_w(S_i v) = \begin{cases} \text{T} & \text{if } S_i v \in h(w), \text{ and for all } \varphi \text{ such that } a_v(\varphi) = \text{T} \\ & a_w(S_i \varphi) \neq \text{F and } a_w(S_i(v \models \varphi)) \neq \text{F}, \\ & \text{and there exists a } w' \text{ such that } a_w(S_i w') = \text{T} \\ & \text{and for all } \varphi \text{ such that } a_v(\varphi) = \text{T}, a_{w'}(\varphi) = \text{T} \\ \text{F} & \text{if } \neg S_i v \in h(w), \text{ and for all } w' \text{ s.t. } a_w(S_i w') = \text{T} \\ & \text{there exists a } \varphi \text{ s.t. } a_v(\varphi) = \text{T and } a_{w'}(\varphi) = \text{F} \\ * & \text{otherwise} \end{cases}$$

We can now add the above (no longer eliminable) definition as an axiom.

23. $S_i v \leftrightarrow \bigwedge_{\varphi \in h(v)} ((v \models \varphi) \rightarrow (S_i \varphi \wedge S_i(v \models \varphi)))$

It should be clear that the resulting logic remains sound. Completeness is a little less obvious. Specifically we must add to the construction of the canonical model and add a case to the truth lemma. First, we must add to the construction of the list of hereditary subformulae of Γ'. We begin with the same construction as before. This will initially give us a list of all the formulae not containing any occurrences of formulae of the form $S_i v$ (for any i and v). At the next stage we add all formulae of that form. We then follow essentially the previous procedure. In other words we add all boolean combinations and quantifications of previously occurring formulae in order of increasing complexity. Once this is done we add all formulae of the form $w \models \varphi$ in the order that φ appeared previously in the list. Finally, we repeat these last two steps alternatively until all of Γ' is exhausted. The remainder of the construction of the canonical model is the same as before.

All that remains to ensure completeness is to check that the truth lemma holds for formulae of the form $S_i v$. In other words we must show that for all i and v, $a_w(S_i v) = \text{T}$ iff $S_i v \in w$.

Proof. Suppose $S_i v \in w$. Then $S_i v \in h(w)$ by definition. And, given φ such that $a_v(\varphi) = \text{T}$, by consistency and axiom 23, $a_w(S_i \varphi) \neq \text{F}$ and $a_w(S_i(v \models \varphi)) \neq \text{F}$. To show that the last criterion for making $a_w(S_i v) = \text{T}$ is satisfied, assume for reductio that there is no w' satisfying $a_v(\varphi) = \text{T} \Rightarrow a_{w'}(\varphi) = \text{T}$ for which it is consistent to make $S_i w'$ true at w. Then, for all w' such that $\neg S_i(w') \in h(w)$ there is some φ such that $a_v(\varphi) = $ T but $a_{w'}(\varphi) = $ F. Since, by definition of h, $\neg S_i v \in h(w)$, if we let v be w', then there is some φ such that $a_v(\varphi) = $ T and $a_v(\varphi) = $ F.

Suppose $a_w(S_i v) = $ T. Then $S_i v \in h(w)$. So, either $S_i v \in w$ or $\neg S_i v \in w$. Suppose $\neg S_i v \in w$. If for all $\varphi \in h(v)$, $((v \models \varphi) \to (S_i(\varphi) \land S_i(v \models \varphi)))$ is consistent with the members of w, then $\neg S_i v$ is not consistent with the members of w by axiom 23. So, there must be some $\varphi \in h(v)$ such that $\neg((v \models \varphi) \to (S_i(\varphi) \land S_i(v \models \varphi)))$ is consistent with the members of w. Let φ_0 be any such formula allowing $\neg S_i v$ into w. By soundness, if $\neg((v \models \varphi_0) \to (S_i(\varphi_0) \land S_i(v \models \varphi_0)))$ is understood at w, it is true there. That would mean that, $a_w(v \models \varphi_0) = $ T and $a_w(S_i \varphi_0) = $ F and $a_w(S_i(v \models \varphi_0)) = $ F, contradicting the assignment $a_w(S_i v) = $ T. □

We thus have a sound and complete logic for representing common knowledge after all.

A goal of this chapter was to set out a formal logic that is expressive enough to finitely capture common knowledge and that is sound and complete. Presumably we have done that. The semantics of our resulting characterization of common knowledge involves nonwellfounded situations and captures the essentials of Barwise's shared-situation approach to common knowledge.

We have done something more than that as well. In setting out the necessary machinery we have produced a logic that captures many features of epistemic awareness. First, we have captured the key aspects of familiarity as discussed in the last two chapters. Second, unlike the logic of chapter 7, this logic captures a more standard epistemic modality than mere familiarity: we do not end up back in classical logic just because all terms are understood. Third, we have captured the finite nature of what is actually known in any given situation, making the logic more cognitively and computationally realistic than more standard epistemic logics. This is not the first logic to represent limited awareness, but it does so based on a world structure that is also epistemic rather than the more usual approach of basing epistemic modality on alethic possible worlds.

Having concluded our study of the formal representation of common knowledge, we now return to the issues that gave rise to it.

10
Convention Revisited

The last several chapters have looked at the structure of common knowledge and at semantics and logics for representing knowledge and common knowledge. Aside from the intrinsic interest such issues hold, we were motivated by the desire to give an account of conditions deemed necessary for convention and/or coordinated action to occur. This in turn was motivated by the desire to give a conventional account of logic that avoided both the vicious regress of explicit conventionalism and the apparent vacuity of as-ifism.

As mentioned in the first chapter, we accept the argument that explicit conventionalism results in vicious regress. Recall that the primary argument there was that there is no way to finitely capture all the infinity of truth assignments necessary to capture logical truth. Thus, there is no way to explicitly set out all the necessary conventions to follow without assuming the ability to make logical inferences from given instructions. We might attempt to challenge this. After all, we have devoted a good deal of this book to the finite representation of things often thought to be only infinitely representable (or thought to presume an infinity). But, while many of the ideas raised herein make it tempting to raise such a challenge, in the end I simply don't know whether it could be successfully maintained. In any case it is unnecessary since there is another avenue open to us.

The view we will defend is one in which the properties of logic are as if it had come about through the adoption of a set of conventions. Let us recall Quine's argument against such a view. He saw no difficulty with as-ifism for ordinary linguistic conventions. In principle, it is often possible to state linguistic conventions before their adoption, even though in practice we "formulate them to fit our behavior." The problem he saw with conventionalism for logic is that it lacks "explanatory force". In the case of logic, it is not possible to state the conventions beforehand. The as-ifism for conventions of logic is not just a feature of historical fact; their as-ifism is essential to their statement. "We may wonder what one adds to the bare statement that the truths of logic and mathematics are a priori, or to the still barer behavioristic statement that they are firmly accepted, when he characterizes them as true by convention in such a sense." (Quine 1936, p. 106) Lest there be any confusion, I reiterate that Quine is not claiming here the impossibility of conventionalism for logic. We saw in the first chapter that Putnam made this misinterpretation. Lewis seems to make essentially the same error.

> [C]onsider this argument given by Quine and others. The first convention of language to be established could not originate by an agreement conducted in a convention-governed language. So even if *any* convention of language could originate by such an agreement, not *all* of them could. ... I offer this rejoinder: an agreement sufficient to create a convention need not be a transaction involving language or any other conventional activity. All it takes is an exchange of manifestations of a propensity to conform to a regularity. These manifestations might simply be displays of conforming action in various appropriate situations, done during a face-to-face meeting in order to create a convention. Such an exchange of displays might be called an "agreement" without stretching the term too far. (Lewis 1969, pp. 87–88)

Actually, it is an overstatement to claim that Lewis has misinterpreted Quine here. This quote is part of a longer discussion of whether conventions require the possibility in principle of originating in agreement. Lewis reasonably finds the arguments on both sides inconclusive. In either case, he takes it to be more significant that conventions in practice need not originate in agreement. And this is unaffected by the outcome of the debate on which origins are possible in principle. We will ultimately find nothing wrong with Lewis's account other than that it did not go far enough for our purposes: he indicates how conventions might arise without even the possibility in principle of explicit linguistic agreement in a convention-governed language, but he does not speak to the utility of such conventions as a basis for logic. Regardless of what Quine intended, another point of real significance for us in his discussion is his questioning of the utility of such conventions. He questions what we gain from a conventional account of logic, and Lewis does not try to answer this. That is not a criticism of Lewis. He is explicating convention first and looking at convention in natural language second. Nowhere in *Convention* does he even raise the issue of a conventional account of logic.

In fact, Quine's argument fits well with the account(s) of convention that Lewis later gave. For, all of these accounts (game-theoretic and otherwise) involve the ability to derive various orders of expectations about the actions of other 'conventioneers'. In fact, all of these accounts assume common knowledge between them, where the order of expectations derivable therefrom is limited not by logic but only by the cognitive abilities of the agents. In other words, these accounts of convention all assume that some logic is presupposed amongst those who would convene, at least once the convention is established; moreover, they assume that logical truths and the ability to reason logically are common knowledge. Thus, Quine's claim that logical behavior is simply what we do seems apropos. Whether or not Quine's question about explanatory utility is a problem for Lewis, it needs to be answered if we are to have a reasonable account of logic as conventional. It appears that the only hope for the essential as-ifism we have described is in the possibility of a different account of convention than those discussed so far. That is one of the primary goals of this chapter.

10.1 Common Knowledge in Conventions

The last paragraph overstated things slightly. Not all of Lewis's characterizations of convention assume common knowledge (of anything). The first one he gives does not require common knowledge (p. 42). However, he quickly adds that requirement and retains it for all remaining accounts. What prompts him to do so? He gives us two reasons (p. 59). First, common knowledge seems to be a feature of all the examples of convention he discusses. Let us grant this reason for the moment. Second, certain behaviors fit the first definition for which the label 'convention' seems counterintuitive.

Lewis's main example of this is one in which everyone drives on the right hand side of the road, and expects everyone else to do so, and prefers to do so in order to prevent collisions (i.e., given that everyone else does so). But, instead of assuming all this to be common knowledge, we assume that everyone holds the false belief that all the others drive on the right purely out of habit and would continue to do so regardless of the behavior of other drivers.

It would be counterintuitive to call the behavior in this example conventional. And, while the requirement of common knowledge rules out such counterintuitive cases, it is not the only way to do so. Recall the first definition that Lewis gives for 'convention':

> A regularity R in the behavior of members of a population P when they are agents in a recurrent situation S is a **convention** if and only if, in any instance of S among the members of P,

1. everyone conforms to R;
2. everyone expects everyone else to conform to R;
3. everyone prefers to conform to R on condition that the others do, since S is a coordination problem and uniform conformity to R is a proper coordination equilibrium in S. (p. 42)

Let us set aside other issues that caused Lewis to modify his definition. That is, let us set aside for the moment that conventional behavior generally occurs between almost everyone in a population rather than everyone, and let us accept that we were correct in chapter 3 when we claimed that all conventions could be characterized via coordination problems. What modifications could we make in the above definition that would rule out counterintuitive cases such as the one just given? Instead of adding common knowledge of the convention requirements, we might amend those requirements. Specifically we might add the following requirement:

4. everyone expects everyone else to prefer to conform to R on condition that the others do, since S is a coordination problem and everyone expects everyone else to prefer uniform conformity to proper coordination equilibria.

It might seem that we have just started our march up the iterated hierarchy of mutual expectations generated by common knowledge and that, with a little ingenuity we can come up with counterintuitive examples that satisfy this definition too. In fact, Lewis points out that we can construct a series of such cases, the second of which is one in which nobody holds the false belief mentioned above but attributes it to everyone else. This case will satisfy the definition, including the requirement just added.

But, even if these odd examples seem to show that we cannot do without common knowledge in principle, there is still something that seems more right about this definition in practice. For, the fact is that we generally do drive to the right out of habit. And, if we expect others to drive to the right, it is not primarily because of any rules or because of any expectations about their rationality but simply because that too is our repeated experience, i.e., a habit. And, the requirement of common knowledge seems necessary only to justify ruling out possibilities of apparently conventional behavior based on rather unconventional beliefs, possibilities that nobody but philosophers (and those who fall under their sophistical spells) take seriously anyway.

Given this it might seem that we should just drop the new requirement and go back to the original definition. However, the added requirement is necessary not merely to rule out anomalous beliefs but also to rule out anomalous counterfactual behaviors. Consider the example in which everyone holds the false belief that all drivers besides himself keep to the right regardless of the behavior of others. Suppose now that a driver is forced to swerve left because a pedestrian suddenly steps into the road. Suppose further that there is an oncoming car, and that it seems clear from the position of the vehicles that the oncoming car can avoid a collision if he too swerves left. (Let us assume that the pedestrian immediately retreated back to the curb.) Nobody would assume that the oncoming driver would continue in his lane if he realized his option in time to act. This is because it is assumed that he prefers to coordinate his actions with others in the face of potential collisions. In other words, the false belief is not just odd; it also fails to agree with ordinary behavior when the apparent convention is violated.

Once we grant this, however, it should be clear that the added requirement is insufficient. For, Lewis's second case would also imply unrealistic behavior in the face of violations of the apparent convention. And examples involving more realistic beliefs are fairly easy to construct. Of course, this should come as no surprise. We saw in chapter 4 that common knowledge was required for coordination, not just for convention. This remains so, despite the fact that in general we drive to the right simply out of habit.

10.2 Habits and Conventions

There is a tension in the role played by common knowledge in convention (and coordination). On the one hand, without it our characterization of convention will not agree with standard behavior or beliefs associated with conventions (or perhaps their violation). On the other hand, conventions often are simply habits in practice. There is some acceptance of this habitual aspect of conventions in Lewis (1969). When discussing conventions born of agreements, he points out that they will not even qualify as conventions until the original agreement ceases to be the primary reason for conforming to the conventional behavior. In fact, the original parties to the agreement may be replaced over time by others who follow the convention in complete ignorance of the agreement. Still Lewis always maintains a mutual awareness and expectation of convening on the part of the conventioneers. Up to the limits of rationality, or at least current introspection, everyone is convening with an understanding of the mutual benefits of convening, of the options in ways of doing so, of the intentions of the others to convene, etc.

So, for Lewis, while people might be acting out of habit, we can characterize their behavior as conventional by considering what they would say they were doing if they thought about it. This applies even when the behavior itself is hard to precisely characterize. Recall the example from Hume of two people rowing a boat smoothly and in a straight line, each with one oar. The physical aspects of the coordinated action may be hard to capture verbally. But, Lewis's account assumes that they would agree with his characterization of their behavior as conventional, up to the limits of their rational abilities. The difference between convention and mere habit (strict conformity to an agreement, etc.) may thus be purely counterfactual. And, we must allow this possibility. Otherwise we have no basis to distinguish between two drivers absent-mindedly going down the right hand side of the road, one of whom would be following the convention (if he thought about it) and the other of whom thinks everyone else drives on the right purely out of habit (when he thinks about this at all).

This necessary tolerance of counterfactual possibilities in conventions, under the characterizations we have been considering, places us on the horns of a dilemma. For, it is easy to construct examples of everyday behavior that seem conventional but for which correctness of the relevant counterfactuals cannot be uniquely determined. The point here is not just that we may not be able to tell for some odd behaviors whether or not they are conventions, but that we must give up either the Lewis characterization of convention or that many of our ordinary conventional behaviors are in fact conventional.

Consider a person who was taught to drive on the right hand side of the road and who knows it's the law and that people generally drive on the right (in the US). Beyond this she has never thought about it at all. Suppose that she drives almost exclusively in the small town where she lives and where she knows virtually every driver she encounters. When asked about her expectations of other drivers she might meet on the road, she naturally assumes that we are talking about people she knows. Against this background we want to know why she drives to the right and expects everyone else to do so.

Consider now some counterfactual situations in which the question would be put to her. Suppose that a local high school boy was recently killed in an accident while speeding and that this is common knowledge in town. In fact everyone has been talking earnestly about the importance of following traffic laws (and emphasizing to their children the importance of doing the right thing regardless of what all the other kids are doing). For whatever reason, discussion on this topic seems to have focussed on kids' disregard of the law, rather than, say, kids' having no common sense. When asked why she drives to the right it is reasonable to assume that our person might well say she does so because it's the law. When asked if everyone else does, she might well say that they do, and they do so because it's the law—plain and simple. Assume that aside from this brief consideration, the matter never comes up for her again.

In another situation there has been no such recent accident, and she recently witnessed her husband break his diet because a bunch of friends wanted to go out for ice cream, which caused her to reflect on what a bunch of sheep live in this town. Under these circumstances she might say that she drives to the right because it's the right thing to do, but everyone else does it just to go along with the crowd. Alternatively, if she's the one who just had a failing of will power she might say that she drives to the right because everyone else does and everyone else does so for the same reasons. As above, let us assume that outside of the brief consideration of driving to the right (in one of these contexts) the matter never comes up for her again.

What are we to say of such a person? How do we decide whether or not her driving on the right is conventional, given her responses in these various counterfactual situations? Should we classify her driving to the right as not conventional unless the first two counterfactual situations are somehow deemed incorrect? I contend that we cannot do so if we hope to count many or even most conventional behaviors as conventional. Furthermore, at the risk of raising a quibble, this concern is based on more realistic counterfactual situations than ones in which someone actually believes that everyone besides himself would drive to the right regardless of what others do.

Another feature of apparent distinction between habit and convention is the existence of alternative behaviors, such as driving to the left instead of the right. Our previous analysis followed Lewis in finding this an important feature of convention. But consider the following example. Suppose that Scott and Louie have been eating lunch together at the Village Deli for some time. They are otherwise constrained so that when they eat lunch is fixed for both of them. They had originally gone in there separately and by coincidence run into one another. After a few chance meetings, however, each of them has made it a point to go there for lunch because he looks forward to seeing the other, and he expects the other to be there. In fact they hold all the requisite mutual expectations and desires for this to amount to a coordination.

Suppose that initially they do not discuss the possibility of meeting elsewhere for lunch. One evening Scott muses to himself that he would be willing to meet Louie at Pancho's Villa for lunch instead, and he wonders whether or not Louie would feel likewise. On a later evening Louie has the same thoughts about meeting Scott at Pancho's. (Their similar tastes make Pancho's a natural candidate for either of them to consider.) About a week after that, one of them mentions Pancho's while they are eating lunch, and it quickly becomes clear that this would be a mutually acceptable alternative. Unfortunately, just one week later Pancho's closes; although neither of them knows this. Some time later, someone mentions the closing to Louie. While he understands this, he does not think to connect this to the possibility of alternative meeting places for lunch with Scott. At some point Scott also finds out that Pancho's is closed. He, however, thinks that the number of desirable luncheon restaurants in town has dwindled to the point that, were it not for the Village Deli, he would just as soon brown bag it and work through lunch in his office. Nonetheless, he does not specifically associate these thoughts with his regular lunches with Louie. He does not think about those lunch meetings at all at the time. He is just thinking generally about restaurant ambiance and other things that concern him in this context. In fact, he soon forgets having heard about Pancho's being closed and what thoughts that had prompted. They continue to meet for lunch at the Village Deli for at least a month after this without any further thought about any of this, other than to go there for lunch at the appropriate time expecting to see the other. Is this a convention? When did it become one? If not, when did it stop?

The problems raised here are not only slippery slope or *sorites* type difficulties. This example raises questions about specific criteria for conventionality at specific points. We could say there is a convention roughly when all the relevant mutual expectations about the Village Deli obtain. The need for an acceptable alternative coordination could then be demonstrated counterfactually. Scott and Louie eventually agreed that Pancho's was acceptable anyway. Were they to have been asked earlier, no doubt they would have agreed. But, what if neither of them would have thought of Pancho's earlier? What if, having not thought of Pancho's, each decided that the Village Deli was the only place he would meet the other? What if, had they been pushed still further, one would have said that he would meet the other anyplace for lunch but that there wasn't anyplace else, while the other would have just said he couldn't imagine wanting to meet anyplace else for lunch? All of these are open, despite the fact that, had Pancho's specifically been mentioned, they would both consider it a viable alternative. Would it matter if Pancho's were closed before they were asked? Would it matter if they knew this, or if they made the relevant connections?

Suppose we find these counterfactual conditions to be clear enough to avoid any problems. Then Scott and Louie meet conventionally once the mutual expectations form. But, the meetings cease to be a convention once Scott considers the possibility that Louie might not be willing to meet other than at the Village Deli. (Unless he doesn't consider this a 'real' possibility?) If this is the case, it becomes conventional again once they make each other aware that there is a mutually acceptable alternative. Does it ever cease to be conventional after this? Once Pancho's closes, they have no mutually acceptable meeting place even though neither of them knows this. What about once Louie knows that Pancho's is closed? His relevant expectations and beliefs about the convention are the same. On the other hand, the options he considers open are not really available. Unless we find either of these points compelling (which I do not) we seem to be forced back to counterfactual reasoning: Louie would realize that there is no given mutually acceptable alternative if he thought about it. But, would he still meet Scott for lunch elsewhere if an acceptable place were suggested? He might not know the answer to this himself even if it were put to him. He may not have sorted out his desires and his notion of acceptable alternatives clearly enough for this to have a determinate answer. Does the answer to this even matter if he cannot think of any acceptable alternatives? We could go on to discuss Scott's beliefs and their role in the convention, but these probably don't raise any theoretical problems not raised by Louie's beliefs in this context.[32]

Perhaps in the spirit of Gettier: suppose that Pancho's only shut down for a week, after they had agreed on it as an acceptable alternative, but neither of them ever heard about it. Was their meeting not conventional that week? What if it had only shut down for a day? Presumably their belief that they could go to Pancho's (other than during that week or day) was true, but it was certainly no more justified the following week than during that week. If it is not justified in general, do we have to check on the availability of our options every time we coordinate in order to maintain conventionality?

The fact is that most conventions are followed without much if any thought about their conventionality. And, the above examples show that there may be no unique set of thoughts about conventionality that the relevant parties would hold, were they to have any. Further, the possible sets may yield knowledge and expectations compatible with Lewis's characterizations, or awareness of a unique coordination equilibrium as such, or no awareness of any coordination equilibrium as such at all. They also show that whether or not an alternative equilibrium

---

[32] Cf. Lewis's discussion of expectation *in sensu diviso* and expectation *in sensu composito*. (Lewis 1969, pp. 64-ff.)

is available, and/or whether or not this is known or determinable, may fail to separate conventional behavior from nonconventional behavior. If the characterizations of convention that we have been considering do not clearly capture ordinary cases, then perhaps we need an alternative.

10.3 Nonmonotonic Situated Convention

A clearer picture of the relevant issues will emerge if we examine the differences between the above examples and Lewis's examples of candidates for conventional behavior that fail to be conventional. Recall the driver who believes that everyone else would drive to the right even if this meant collisions. An important difference between his situation and that of the woman in the small town is that it is impossible to embed his beliefs in a context giving rise to a convention in the Lewis sense. That is, no matter how much rationality or how many other beliefs we add, it is clear that the situation he is in could not yield a Lewis convention (unless he relinquished the very belief that characterizes the situation). It is hard to imagine any ordinary situation in which such a belief could arise; nonetheless it is part of the given situation. However, in the case of the woman in the small town the basic situation description was one for which we could construct more detailed counterfactual situations with important differences. In at least one of them her beliefs were consistent with a conventional account of driving behavior and in other counterfactual situations her beliefs were not thus consistent.[33]

---

[33]Even in the situations where her beliefs were inconsistent with a conventional account it seems intuitive to say that her beliefs were revisable in a way that was not available to the drivers Lewis described. In the first situation we imagined for our small town driver, circumstances naturally prompted her to say that everyone drives to the right because it's the law. Suppose, however, that she were prompted further. Specifically, suppose she were asked if she really believed that anyone in town would continue driving to the right and risk collisions even if everybody else in town were driving on the left. It is far more plausible to think that she would agree to the conventionality of the situation, if it were put in these terms, than that she would continue to insist that the law is the only reason for the behavior. Indeed, were she to continue to insist on this we would probably be inclined to view her as somewhat pathological. If we had reason to believe she really meant it, for example, if she caused an accident by staying right in a case where going left would clearly have avoided the accident, then we would have reason to believe that her driving to the right was not conventional after all.

Perhaps because in Lewis's example it is hard to imagine any ordinary situation in which such a belief could arise, it seems that the belief must be accepted as a given in the situation. However, in the case of the woman in the small town it is easy to conceive of additional information consistent with the basic situation description that would cause her to revise her opinion. These points are only vaguely expressed here and a more detailed treatment would take us away from our main concerns. For

Similar considerations apply to the restaurant example. It seems not to matter whether or not Pancho's is closed or how aware Scott and Louie are of this and its connection to their situation. The reason is that, for virtually all of the scenarios we considered for them, it is possible to conceive of an embedding of that situation in one where their meeting is conventional. We never rule out the possibility that they each could believe that they could meet elsewhere for lunch.

It thus appears that only a minor revision of the characterization of convention is required. We don't require, as before, that a regularity R in the behavior of members of a population P when they are agents in a recurrent situation S be a convention if and only if, in any instance of S among the members of P the appropriate conditions are met. Rather, we require that any instance of S be a subsituation of a situation S' in which those conditions are met. Specifically, in S' amongst some members of P it must be common knowledge amongst them that they are in situation S' and that in any instance of S'

1. everyone conforms to R;
2. everyone expects everyone else to conform to R;
3. everyone prefers to conform to R on condition that the others do, since S' is a coordination problem and uniform conformity to R is a proper coordination equilibrium in S'.

(We are ignoring here that the conditions for conventions need be met only by most of the members of a population rather than all.)

This characterization is nonmonotonic because a given situation may be extended in such a way that the extension is no longer a subsituation of any situation satisfying the above conditions. This may seem too broad. It encompasses any behavioral regularity occurring in a recurrent situation amongst member of a population in which those who are engaging in the convention are not thinking or doing anything to specifically render it not conventional. (Recall our discussion in section 6.2 of common knowledge in the coordinated attack.) Two people absent-mindedly smiling as they walk past each other every morning ends up being a convention on our account. But, a moments reflection should tell us that this is exactly what we want.

---

work on belief revision cf., e.g., Gärdenfors 1988. Other related work is mentioned in Ginsberg 1987. Cf. esp. the "Yale shooting problem".

11

Conventions in Logic

11.1 Convening without Common Knowledge

Two problems remain for a conventional account of logic. We must demonstrate its utility, and we must show how we could arrive at conventional logic without prior common knowledge of logic. The former problem will be dealt with in a later section, the latter in this one.

As Quine noted, conventions of logic could only be specified after their adoption. Thus, the common knowledge of behavioral regularities as coordination equilibria (necessary for coordination to take place) are only available for logical conventions ex post facto. It is thus difficult to see how the conventions could be arrived at in the first place. A partial answer was already given by Lewis, and we have quoted it above. Namely, "an agreement sufficient to create a convention need not be a transaction involving language or any other conventional activity. All it takes is an exchange of manifestations of a propensity to conform to a regularity. These manifestations might simply be displays of conforming action in various appropriate situations, done during a face-to-face meeting in order to create a convention."

Thus, during the prehistory of a convention, it need not even be the case that the prospective participants recognize a behavior as regular, either in others or themselves, much less that this be common knowledge between them. A behavior can be learned by repeated exposure. In fact a person can repeat a behavior even if he doesn't know what he did. This is a common experience in learning, with or without a teacher. Once the behavior itself is recognized it is easy enough to build evidence for coordination by a repeated "exchange of manifestations of a propensity to conform to a regularity". We can bootstrap our way to convention just as the two generals were able to bootstrap their way to common knowledge in chapter 4.

By itself, this argument might seem inadequate because it is too speculative. It is one thing for such conventions to arise in the case of Hume's rowers, for example. The rowers might simply recognize that when their strokes synchronize they move more smoothly and evenly. They could then fall into attempts to synchronize and eventually to maintain this. The convention would become simply to row 'thus'. But, when we are talking about logic, things are trickier. It is at the least hard to imagine speakers of some nonlogical language experimenting with inference and falling into regularities. Partly this is because, as Quine is so fond of pointing out, logic is in effect imposed on a language. A nonlogical natural language would presumably be impossible in his eyes. But this only strengthens our case. If one believes the most basic aspects of evolutionary science, then one must accept that humans (i.e., the only uncontroversially and widely accepted users of language) developed from simpler non-language-users. Unless logico-linguistic ability either arose instantaneously and spontaneously or developed only through biological evolution and never through learning and experience within individuals, then something like the above must have occurred.

We saw above in chapters 3 through 6 that solutions to coordination problems require something like common knowledge. This is consistent with the idea in game theory that assuming common knowledge of the available strategies and outcomes of all players allows us to account for equilibria. This is actually a little too restrictive a claim. The type of equilibria we looked at in chapters 2 and 3 are generally known as Nash equilibria. Game theorists have found Nash equilibria to be unsatisfactory (both as too narrow and too broad) for capturing some behaviors. Various other types of equilibria have been studied (Bernheim 1984, Pearce 1984, Selten 1988). And, depending on the type of equilibrium, the common knowledge involved may vary (Tan and Werlang 1988a,b; Aumann 1992). Nonetheless, for all types of equilibria, at minimum it is assumed that all players have common knowledge that the other players are rational in some specific sense.[34] If common knowledge of rationality in some minimal sense is necessary for coordination on any type of equilibrium, then there must be something wrong with our story in which a convention could arise through demonstrations of a propensity to conform to a regularity, even if we cannot say what is wrong. At

---

[34] There are problems in economic contexts with common knowledge of rationality, strategies, payoffs, etc. Many of these stem from the problem that under these circumstances, if every two party economic transaction has some inherent costs, any transaction that would be rational for one party would not be for the other (Aumann 1976, Moses and Nachum 1990, Geanakopolos 1992). There are also some games that have solutions only if certain things are not common knowledge (Bicchieri 1988). While closely related, none of this affects the results we discuss here.

least this development of conventions could not apply to logical conventions since these would presumably be constituents of that minimal rationality.

There are a number of adequate responses to this concern. First, all the appeals to common knowledge we have looked at so far amount to inferences to the best explanation. We have found cases where failure to coordinate can be associated with a failure of common knowledge. And, it has been proven that common knowledge of certain conditions goes hand in hand with certain types of equilibria—in the sense that those equilibria are the only n-tuples of strategies (in an n person game) consistent with common knowledge (Tan and Werlang 1988b). Common knowledge thus seems to be a reasonable basis for convention. But, is it really required for coordination? Especially given the idealizations that traditional accounts of common knowledge can involve, it may be reasonable to say that we find the explanation wanting, even if we have nothing to offer in its place.

Second, we can offer at least one alternative to common knowledge as an explanation for game equilibria. In the last few decades there has been increasing interest in evolutionary games (Samuelson 1997). These can be directly associated with characterizations of biological evolution (Maynard Smith 1982; Thomas 1984, chap. 8). The basic idea is to think not of players in a game, but of populations interacting—such as a population of predators and a population of prey. Various subpopulations approach interaction via different strategies. Subpopulations playing strategies that are most successful will be most likely to be able to reproduce. Thus, we can associate the average payoff of a strategy with the average fitness of the individuals playing that strategy. ('Fitness' is defined as the expected value of the number of offspring for an individual.)

> Thus one may write a bimatrix in which the rows and columns represent the various possible genetic endowments of the two respective species .... If one views this bimatrix as a game, then the Nash equilibria of this game correspond precisely to population equilibria; that is, under asexual reproduction, the proportions of the various genetic endowments within each population remain constant from generation to generation if and only if these proportions constitute a Nash equilibrium. (Aumann 1992)

The important thing about such a game for our purposes is that there is no need for common knowledge of anything. Indeed there is no knowledge of any kind. For, instead of players, we have interacting populations. Even if we view the populations as players in some broad sense, still they do not choose strategies. It is the selection process that determines the strategies the 'players' will follow. Equilibria arise without any prior mutual expectation on anyone's part. In other words, even if the 'players' might be technically said to have common knowledge in virtue of the equilibria, there is nobody who forms any sort of expectations in order for those equilibria to arise.[35]

11.2 Conventional Signals

Both of the above points are telling, but perhaps the best response is to simply question whether minimal rationality implies acceptance of logic. Such a view requires a highly idealized concept of agent. An agent may not accept all that is logical or even all that is logically implied (in the classical sense) by some of his beliefs. This much is in keeping with our discussions in previous chapters. But, even in chapter 9 we were considering somewhat idealized agents. Cherniak (1986) argues that once we "begin to take into account at least the most basic facts of an agent's psychological reality, ..., not only is acceptance of a metatheoretically adequate [sound and complete] deductive system not transcendentally indispensable for an agent's rationality; in important cases it is inadvisable and perhaps even incompatible with that rationality" (p. 99). He cites a wide range of recent evidence that people do not use formally correct methods in their intuitive reasoning. (And he argues that they should not, from a practical standpoint.) We need not look at his arguments in detail for our purposes. On an intuitive level it is hard to see why minimally rational agents could not agree on illogical conventions. This is a lesson that anyone who has taught elementary logic classes should have learned from his students.

So far in this chapter, we have been trying to make sense of applying coordination and convention concepts to the development of logic, but we have said little on the positive side: little about how such conventions might have more specific properties that more naturally describe them. We have noted previously, in chapter 5, that conventional coordinations require a good deal of action. What sort of action might this be in a prelogical agent? Any answer must of course be speculative. It is conceivable that an agent B does some action $action_2$, whenever another A does $action_1$. Observing this, agent A might get the idea that if he does $action_1$, then B does $action_2$. We do not pretend that

---

[35]For a limited class of games, Samuelson has also shown that the type of equilibrium that a game has is determined by properties of the evolutionary process. Thus, the kinds of things that end up being common knowledge between players, can be explained by the evolutionary process affecting the game. Perfect equilibria (those requiring the largest amount of common knowledge) occur precisely when the evolutionary process yields a single pattern of behavior (Samuelson 1988).

this is sufficient for a conventional idea of (any) conditional: there is no generalization to other such connections, there is no indication of what happens when A does not do $action_1$, etc. Most importantly, there is no convention as yet of any kind. A and B would have to form a mutual expectation and understanding around these actions. Still one can imagine such actions in elaborate and varied enough situations giving rise to logical conventions of action without any explicit recognition of them by those convening. One could imagine this if there were no confusions, no errors, no violations. But, as we have noted, this does not happen even when a logic is explicitly available. It is possible that individual agents will not ever adapt to any logic. All logical convention arises in such a population via the evolution of the population itself. In this case we would have a population that behaves logically but does not have logic, at least not in the sense that we do.

To be capable of giving rise to an understanding of logic—an expectation of logic rather than just specific behaviors that outsiders to the population would recognize as logical—it would thus seem that individual members of the population must be able to recognize ambiguities, errors, and the like. As we have discussed, convention involves expectation, values, and payoffs. And, there needs to be a desire or at least propensity to act consistent with coordination equilibria. We could perhaps consistently explain individual awareness of some aspects of logic while still maintaining that the only reinforcement of the coordination equilibria that constitute logical conventions is via reproductive fitness pressure within the population. But, it is both more intuitive and simpler to assume that individuals with an ability to recognize conventional logical behavior also have the ability reinforce that behavior. In other words, they can indicate to each other a propensity to follow them. If this is right, then such individuals are capable of what Lewis called *signaling*.

As with other conventional behaviors, Lewis (1969) described signaling game-theoretically. In a signaling game, there is a *sender* and an *audience*. This seems to imply a single agent doing the sending and a set of agents doing the receiving, a natural way to view things. But, the sending of a signal might itself involve the combined actions of several agents or sending might ignore whether something is sent redundantly by several agents. And, there may only be a single member of the audience. For simplicity's sake, we will abstract away from these issues and view signaling as a two-person game involving a *sender* and a *receiver*. The sender sends messages in various situations. The sender has a strategy for what message to send in various situations, and the receiver has a strategy of what action to take depending on the message received. If, for each situation, the action taken by the receiver is preferred by both over any other action for that situation, then the result is a *signaling system*.

Lewis (1969) has a good deal to say about signals and signaling systems, especially in the analysis of language. We will not recount any of that here. We limit ourselves to a few observations. Signaling here implies guaranteed communication. We make this point because it might seem otherwise given our longest running example, that of the two generals. At least as we have described them, they do not have a signaling system because a sender could send without the receiver receiving. If one wished to do so, probably the best way to think of the two generals in terms of signaling systems is as a composition of signaling systems in which there are three agents, the two generals and the environment between them. Sometimes each of these is the sender, sometimes the receiver. We leave it to the interested reader to try to describe the coordinated attack in terms of signaling systems. A more important observation is that, unlike the case of the generals, in establishing conventions of logic the meaning of the messages may be unclear. Or they may even be unspecified outside the signaling system.

Realizing this it may be surprising or thought a lucky coincidence that conventions of meaningful communication could arise. However, Wäneryd (1993) showed that this is not entirely true. Of the Nash equilibria that might occur in an evolutionary setting, there is a more resilient class of *evolutionarily stable strategies* (ESS), (Maynard Smith and Price 1973, Maynard Smith 1982). An ESS is an equilibrium that will be maintained even if some small proportion of the population follows a mutant strategy. What Wäneryd (1993) showed was that in signaling games with coincidence of interest, only signaling systems are evolutionarily stable. Given this, it is less surprising that there are clearly lots of non-human users of signaling systems, whatever opinion we may have of whether or not there are non-human users of either logic or language. And it is not just primates or even mammals. One of the more well-known examples is the dance that honey bees do to indicate to hive mates the direction and distance of a source of nectar.

11.3 Getting to Logic

We have seen how a convention could arise without prior common knowledge of the conditions for a convention. We have yet to answer Quine's question of what role a conventional view of logic has to play. The answer is that it provides a more plausible accounting of logical behavior than simply saying that the truths of logic are "firmly accepted". For this gives us no explanation of how or why they are firmly accepted. A conventional account of logic gives us both. That is, it gives us a plausible story of how logical behavior might have come about. Admittedly, our above account of convention does not give anything more than a broad framework on which the details of the development of logical conventions could be hung. It does not provide any account of the development of the conventional acceptance of a single logical truth or adopting of a single logical behavior. And, such an account might never be given. Indeed, it is hard to imagine that evidence will ever be available that will demonstrate a transition from some proto-language to a language exhibiting logical properties. None of this matters. Such evidence would be nice to have, but in its absence we still have a rather plausible theory of the development of logic. Without a better proposal, or at least some substantive and sustainable criticism of the theory, there is little ground for rejecting it as empty. In fact, the main difficulty with the theory was the highly ideal rationality (and mutual understanding) that convention—and coordination in general—seems to imply. But, we have seen that this implication was merely apparent.

This point is to me quite powerful and an adequate answer in itself. For this reason the last paragraph is unchanged from when it was first written nearly a decade ago. However, we can speculate a bit more about how specifically some parts of logic can arise. In fact, Skyrms (2000) does just that. Skyrms builds on certain signaling systems used by vervet monkeys and described by Cheney and Seyfarth (1990).

Vervets are prey to several kinds of predators: principally leopards, snakes, and eagles. They give distinct alarm calls in response to each of these. And, the response of others around them varies based on the call that is heard. In response to a leopard call, they typically climb up trees. In response to a snake call, they typically stand erect and gaze about on the ground. When it is spotted, monkeys gather around it from a safe distance, while repeating the snake call. In response to an eagle call, they typically look in the sky and sometimes run into the bushes. If they are in trees when an eagle call is heard, they will scan the sky but may also climb down and go under bushes (Cheney and Seyfarth 1990). Vervets also have other calls that occur in various circumstances, including some associated with lesser predatory threats.

Skyrms (2000) speculates how agents such as these might come to develop "proto-truth functions". Suppose that a vervet is sometimes able to detect evidence of a predator but not the exact kind of predator. For example, motion in the grass might imply either a leopard or a snake. Presumably the optimal response to such an ambiguous circumstance might be different from one where there is clearly a leopard or clearly a snake. "One would not want to stumble on the snake while running for the nearest tree to escape the leopard. One would not want to draw a leopard's attention by standing up straight and scanning the ground for snakes.... Then, the evolutionary (or learning) dynamics would be no different than the one we would have if we had four predators, four messages, and four appropriate evasive actions in the original story." (Skyrms 2000, pp. 85–86) This Skyrms considers to be a proto-truth function. He does not think that the monkeys must recognize it as truth functional and acknowledges that it could also be given the meaning, e.g., terrestrial predator.

If the agents we are considering (presumably not vervets) are capable of many such proto-truth functions, then we can begin to have inference, e.g., when one signals snake-or-leopard and another signals not-leopard at the same time. Either via learning or reproductive selection it is easy to see the evolutionary advantage of a receiver that responds optimally for a snake rather than a snake-or-leopard under these circumstances (Skyrms 2000, p. 86).

True enough, but negation seems like a hard one to explain, and Skyrms simply assumes the agents have such a signal without the story he gave for 'or'. A couple of possibilities can be gleaned from Cheney and Seyfarth (1990). Young vervets give erroneous predator calls. The very young give an eagle call for numerous birds of both raptor and non-raptor species, including species that are not a threat even to infant vervets. Older juveniles are better about this distinction but not as good as adults at giving the call only when species of eagles that actually prey on them are sighted. In response to incorrect calls, adults typically look up and then return to what they are doing. In response to correct calls, adults typically look up and give the call themselves. This can reinforce learning in juveniles. However, there is apparently no evidence that the adults are attempting to teach or correct juvenile error (*op. cit.*, pp. 129–ff.). There are also instances in which vervets appear to give false alarm calls intentionally. Perhaps the most interesting case is when a subordinate male vervet encountered an outside male attempting to join its group. This male had a history of being dominated by other males joining his group. When encountering an approaching outsider male, he gave the leopard alarm. This caused the other to run up a tree and thus delayed his approach to the group. However, on more than one occasion the 'liar' would get down from a tree he was in and cross to another tree closer to the interloper. He apparently did not recognize the inconsistency in giving the leopard alarm and leaving a tree to walk across open ground. In both of these cases, one can easily imagine the advantages of being able to express negation, whether or not vervets seem capable of it.

Smaller leaps to inference are also conceivable. For example, if two agents issued at the same time a snake-or-leopard and snake-or-lesser-predator call, then we again have the selection pressure in favor of responding to a snake. As in Skyrms example, this assumes that both of the calls are associated with the same predator. And, it is implicit that the 'or' here is exclusive. If the agents in question occasionally face circumstances in which multiple species of predators are present as well as the usual single predator, then we can imagine another story in which there is an optimal response to, e.g., a snake and an eagle that would not be optimal against either one in isolation. None of this adds anything conclusive to the points raised in the first paragraph of this section. However, a story that is consistent with and extends known primate behavior in a plausible way adds a vivid reinforcement to those points.

Another developmental counter to Quine's view can be given by questioning one of his premises. The vacuity he claims for an implicitly conventional account of logic depends on the unavailability of alternatives—i.e., on the viciousness of any explicit account. We saw above that agreement to follow logical conventions seems to require the previous adoption of the very conventions that one is agreeing to follow. That was the trap in which the Tortoise caught Achilles. However, the agreement to follow any one convention does not require its previous adoption. Given an expressive enough metalanguage we could always agree to infer from statements of some form to a conclusion, even if this inference was not previously accepted, either explicitly or implicitly. We can simply agree to reason thus. This does indeed place us in a vicious justificatory regress, but the regress it implies for development of conventions is not vicious. There is nothing wrong in principle with such a characterization of our logical conventions. It presumes the acceptance of some logic in order for there to be an agreement to follow any new logical convention. But, there is nothing vicious in the assumption of an infinite chain of the acceptances (and rejections) of logical conventions without any first element. On this view, all logical conventions could have been explicitly agreed to prior to their adoption whether or not this was actually done. This view does not provide us with a justification of logic, but it does provide us with a story of its firm acceptance—as Quine put it. Of course, this account is unacceptable, but not because it is flawed in principle or because it adds nothing to a bare behavioral description of logic. Rather, it is unacceptable because it is not consistent with everything else we would like to accept.

Specifically it is not consistent with a view of the world in which at one time there was no community of reasoners around to adopt new logical conventions.

11.4 The Utility of Conventionalism

We have shown how logic can arise through convention—and shown this view to fit well with known aspects of human reasoning, coordination, game theory, evolutionary theory, and even animal behavior. That alone should suffice for the utility of conventionalism. But, having shown how to get to logic, we have said precious little about where we have got to, i.e., conventions of logic itself, especially the logic of logicians.

While the account of logic given at the end of the last section is ultimately unacceptable it does recognize something that Quine nowhere seems to acknowledge. There is no corpus of logic that has been accepted through the ages. It is not just that prior to the development of first order logic nobody had thought about the characterization of logical truth or logical consequence. In the *Prior Analytics* Aristotle argued that any deductive argument can be expressed as a series of syllogistic inferences. Even if he was wrong, he still engaged in metalogical analysis and came up with a different system than the one Quine takes to be a priori and firmly accepted. One could make the claim that such people in the history of logic did not have the advantages of the eventual developments that we now understand. While such a move is certainly dubious or at least requiring of some very careful articulation, we will not bother to dispute it. For, there is good empirical evidence that is not subject to this criticism.

Intuitionistic logics reject the law of the excluded middle. Quantum logics reject distribution. Relevance logics reject the validity of Positive Paradox ($\varphi \to (\psi \to \varphi)$). All of these logics were specifically formulated as alternatives to classical logic. There are of course others. The important thing is that they call into question the firm acceptance of any one logic, and they do so in a particularly significant way. First of all, these were developed after first order logic had been developed and even largely after it was found to be sound and complete. The brilliant-historical-predecessors-struggling-in-ignorance maneuver is thus not available to us here. Second, whether or not the views of the logicians who adopt such 'deviant' logics are correct is not the only important issue here. It is also important for us that they think they are correct.

Some logics, e.g., quantum logic, are typically intended to apply to a domain of discourse different from that of natural language descriptions of ordinary experience. It may be that there is no logic adequate for the entirety of even ordinary discourse. If this is true, then the Quinean is more vexed than the conventionalist. The conventionalist can argue that within respective domains, reasoners use the logic that they will. However, the conventionalist can give an account of how this is possible, how it could arise that reasoning in these different contexts follows different logics. And, as we have seen, he does not have to appeal to some prior rationality for this to make sense. The Quinean is forced to choose. He can appeal to some meta-level logic by which reasoners choose which logic to use and which must be outside the domain of ordinary logic, hence essentially ineffable. (If it is effable, then it becomes possible to give a single logic again, just with contextual parameters that reasoners can discern and explicitly choose between.) His only alternative is to essentially fall back on the vacuous, "that's just how we reason".

So, let us restrict ourselves to debates within a single domain of discourse, whether that be mathematics, ordinary experience, the logic of natural language, or all of the above. Quine is not unaware of alternatives to classical logic. It is instructive to see what he has said about them. In the chapter entitled "Deviant Logics" in Quine 1970 he discusses alternatives in general and intuitionistic logics in particular. On the general score he considers what logic is imposed on translation from a strange language. He says that in construing a native speaker of that language we "impute our orthodox logic to him, or impose it on him, by translating his language to suit" (*op. cit.*, p. 82). This is because we cannot reasonably construe the speaker of the other language as contradicting the obvious. "But on this score logic is peculiar: every logical truth is obvious, actually or potentially". Thus, "[t]he canon 'Save the obvious' bans any manual of translation that would represent the foreigners as contradicting our logic (apart from corrigible confusions in complex sentences)." Throughout his discussion Quine makes it clear that he assumes there is one generally accepted logic in ordinary usage. What of the deviants?

Quine agrees, for example, that one can "coherently challenge the classical true-false dichotomy" for sentences. But, he questions why one would want to do so. He notes a number of possible motivations, making his most detailed comments on those from constructive mathematics. He acknowledges that "constructivism, in some such sense, is congenial and admirable. Adherence to constructivist restraints makes for enhanced understanding of what we manage to accomplish within those restraints. Moreover, the paradoxes of set theory put an added premium on constructivism; for what we accomplish within those constraints is pretty clearly immune to the threat of contradiction that lingers outside." (*ibid.*, p. 88) But, he then goes on to describe a 'constructive' set theory that "can be reconciled with the convenience and beauty of classical logic." And concludes that "one can practice and even preach a very considerable degree of constructivism without adopting intuitionistic logic." This is the whole of his response in Quine 1970 to the intuitionist.

Now Quine is far from alone in adopting a compatibilist approach to constructive mathematics. Few would deny that constructive results are generally more illuminating of what they prove than their nonconstructive counterparts; however, the absence of a constructive proof is not taken as vitiating validity. But, for the true believer in intuitionism (of which there are many) it is not just a matter of convenience or added assurance. They claim not to understand logic as classically expressed. They find some of the arguments to be invalid. What of Quine's 'obvious' logical truths? It is odd, to say the least, to claim that some of the greatest logicians of the twentieth century were unable to grasp what is so obvious that we must translate a foreign language as respecting it on pain of construing foreigners as irrational. The general sense of deviant logics that one gets from Quine's discussion is that they are often motivated by genuine concerns in the abstruse technical regions of mathematics and science, but that they amount to overreactions to these concerns. As long as there is some way to deal with these concerns that respects classical logic, Quine cannot see why anyone would do otherwise. Logical truths are, as a group, the most obvious, most incorrigible of all for him. He seems to find it hard to know what it would mean to question them.

The problem is that 'our logic' is a misnomer even for those schooled in twentieth century mathematics and analytic philosophy. While it may apply to a majority of such people, there is a substantial minority to whom it does not apply. And, they are not entirely motivated by mathematical or scientific arcana. Works on relevance logic generally take their examples from everyday speech rather than technical reasoning. The professed goal of such researchers is to give an account of valid inference,[36] not to deal with technical arcana. (Although they produce a fair amount of technical arcana to do so.)

What a conventional account of logic explains that Quine does not is how these deviant logicians can disagree with him on such matters. For, Quine's only avenue is to label them irrational in the sense that

---

[36]It may be interesting to note that Quine's idea of logical quintessence is logical truth, but for intuitionists and relevantists it is generally consequence or valid inference.

they cannot grasp the implicitly obvious even when it is painstakingly explained to them. Wrong they may be. But, it is a very high price to pay to label them irrational. And, the only benefit we gain for paying that price is to avoid adopting conventionalism, the only outstanding objection to which was its lack of explanatory utility. On the conventionalist account it is easy enough to say that these various logicians are simply conforming to different conventions. It is at best unclear that the nonlogician conforms to any single set of logical conventions. Even if he does, contra Quine, there is no general consensus amongst logicians what those conventions are. Thus, conventionalism yields a far more plausible account of logical behavior than simply claiming that it is just what we do (except for those of us who don't).

Quine finishes his essay by saying of the thesis that logic proceeds "wholly from linguistic conventions, only further clarification can assure us that this asserts anything at all". I hope that we have provided here enough clarification to yield that assurance.

11.5 Whither Truth?

Perhaps we have succeeded in giving a coherent conventionalist account of logic. And, perhaps it is free of vicious regress. Perhaps it is even a better account of logical behavior than can be given without conventionalism. Nonetheless, our account seems to retain one feature that makes it unpalatable to many: it commits us to relativity of logical truth. For if the account takes logic, including logical truth, to be conventional, then it must accept the possibility of different sets of logical truths. And, for many objectivity is a *sine qua non* for truth, presumably all the more so for the quintessential type of truth—logical truth. However, contrary to appearance, such a view is compatible with our conventionalism.

Recall the Carnapian notion of logical convention with which we began. There are different ways we can proceed in setting out a logic. On his view there are three things to be given: formation rules of the language, transformation rules, and an interpretation. Not surprisingly, what we do first constrains what comes later. The expressiveness of the language limits the richness of the semantics. And, in the order just mentioned, interpretations should respect the inference rules. Even, e.g., in the case of nonmonotonic logics, they still must conform to the transformation rules in whatever way and by whatever criterion we set: if there is no notion even roughly related to soundness then it is unclear what the interpretation has to do with the inference rules given. Of course we can give an interpretation first; then it is the inference rules that must respect the interpretation. We could even put the language last to some extent by treating all sentences as initially atomic from a logical point of view. We then fix an interpretation and inference rules, in either order, and carve out any logical vocabulary we can that respects those.[37]

It may be that one feels even here that there is a right order. For example Dummett (1973) argues that justification must ultimately come from the semantics. Thus, the interpretation is prior, although not before the formation rules: "there can be no analysis of inferences without a prior analysis of the structure of statements that can serve as premisses and conclusion" (Dummett 1991, p. 2). However, from our perspective this order does not matter. Our primary focus has been to make sense of how people came to say what follows from what without already knowing the answer to that. Whether what ultimately arose did so in the right way is a question that could only be asked afterward, that is in the presence of one or more existing logics. At that point it's easy—not the answer to the question, but a conventionalist account of what's happening. For, once we have a logic, we can argue for the adoption of explicit changes or revisions. Here too we see the advantage of conventionalism. Ultimately somebody may or may not be right in these arguments, but conventionalism gives us an account of acceptable reasoning. 'Acceptable' could be defined by survey of some population or by which papers get accepted for publication. Conventionalism does not say what is right but only what is conventional. It may be that some previously accepted logical features of language are just the opposite of the conventions that we 'know to be true today'. This does not make them any the less conventional. It also does not mean that we must relinquish logical standards. If some fallacy is a violation of logical standards, even if it is commonly enough committed that we might call it conventional, we can still call it a fallacy and say why it is wrong. But, we should recognize that if those be academic, technical standards, then they are themselves conventional (if they are actually accepted standards).

Our conventionalism can even offer an account of those logicians who, like Quine or Dummett, feel that theirs is the one true logic. For we have seen examples of coordination in which there was no actual common knowledge of alternatives to the equilibrium reached, either before or after the coordination took place. Of course we have a problem explaining how they are unable to see those alternatives even when the alternatives are set out for them. There are two possible answers.

---

[37] Thanks to Anthony Everett for pointing out this possibility.

On the one hand, they may be right. This does not preclude, however, the basic game-theoretic picture we hold. It just so happens that external constraints make it such that there is only one right way to coordinate. Conventionalism is apparently precluded because there is no alternative way to coordinate. But, we are then back to the problem of how those who don't accept the one true logic are able to function and coordinate their reasoning with others so well.

It could be argued that they do not actually function well. Perhaps there are very subtle contradictions in their logic(s). Of course this assumes that an inconsistent or paraconsistent logic could not count as an alternative. And, that cannot be justified except by a circular argument. Further, some alternatives may be distinguished by rejecting some truths or inferences of the 'true' logic rather than by accepting some that it rejects. (This is the case for some of the most thoroughly studied alternatives to classical logic.) These may be undesirable because they cannot allow the derivation of rational inferences. For example, a standard classical charge against intuitionism is that it cannot support the mathematical and scientific reasoning of mathematicians and scientists. But, from the perspective of such an alternative, the 'true' logic is the irrational one. The alternative practitioner can baldly reject the 'invalid' inferences. Another possibility is for him to somehow encompass the 'fallacies' to which the opposing logic owes its appeal. He need not go so far as to accept the logic he previously opposed; he may minimally revise his logic or might not even revise his logic at all. He can account for the 'fallacy' by showing what he sees as the correct reasoning to which it owes its appeal, e.g., (γ)-admissibility arguments as one part of the response of relevance logicians to disjunctive syllogism (Anderson and Belnap 1975). Each of these sorts of responses is fairly common, not just in philosophical logic, but also in revision of the rules of other sciences.

Similarly, if the alternative involves an expansion, contraction, or even just overlap with the language of the 'true' logic, it will be hard to give a nonvicious argument why it does not count as a genuine alternative. In the end, even if there is only one true logic, all we can say of the empirically given alternatives is that they are the wrong options to choose; we cannot deny that they are options at all.

On the other hand, those who believe that they are following the one true logic may be wrong. In this case, they fail to clearly recognize the game they are playing. On some level they do recognize the game; even Quine recognizes that there is nothing in principle wrong with some of these deviant logics. But, he retains the basic underlying assumption that there is ultimately only one logic, and this causes him to reject the alternatives as real alternatives. There is no a priori way of knowing which view on the existence of a unique true logic is correct. One may be able to give reasons for labeling one or more alternatives rational and the others irrational. Doing so is independent of the conventionalist account we have given. But, in the absence of such reasons, it is of this labeling that we should wonder whether it asserts anything at all.

References

Anderson, Alan Ross and Nuel D. Belnap. 1975. *Entailment: The Logic of Relevance and Necessity, Volume I*. Princeton University Press.

Aumann, Robert. 1976. Agreeing to Disagree. *Annals of Statistics* 4(6):1236–1239.

Aumann, Robert. 1992. Perspectives on Bounded Rationality. In *Theoretical Aspects of Reasoning about Knowledge: Proceedings of the Fourth Conference*, pages 108–117. San Mateo, California: Morgan Kaufmann.

Barwise, Jon. 1989a. On the Model Theory of Common Knowledge. In *The Situation in Logic*, vol. 17 of *CSLI Lecture Notes*, chap. 9, pages 201–220. Stanford: CSLI Publications.

Barwise, Jon. 1989b. *The Situation in Logic*, vol. 17 of *CSLI Lecture Notes*. Stanford: CSLI Publications.

Barwise, Jon. 1989c. Situations, Facts, and True Propositions. In *The Situation in Logic*, vol. 17 of *CSLI Lecture Notes*, chap. 10, pages 221–254. Stanford: CSLI Publications.

Barwise, Jon and John Perry. 1983. *Situations and Attitudes*. Cambridge, Mass.: MIT Press/Bradford Books.

Bencivenga, Ermanno. 1986. Free Logics. In D. Gabbay and F. Guenthner, eds., *Handbook of Philosophical Logic, vol. III: Alternatives to Classical Logic*, vol. 166 of *Synthese Library*, chap. III.6, pages 373–426. D. Reidel.

Bernheim, B. Douglas. 1984. Rationalizable Strategic Behavior. *Econometrica* 52(4):1007–1028.

Bicchieri, Cristina. 1988. Knowledge and Backward Induction: A Solution to the Paradox. In *Proceedings of the Second Conference on Theoretical Aspects of Reasoning about Knowledge*, pages 381–393. Los Altos, California: Morgan Kaufmann.

Black, Max. 1970a. Justification of the Logical Axioms. In *Margins of Precision*. Ithaca, N.Y.: Cornell University Press.

Black, Max. 1970b. Reasoning with Loose Concepts. In *Margins of Precision*. Ithaca, N.Y.: Cornell University Press.

Bonanno, Giacomo and Klaus Nehring. 2000. Intersubjective consistency of knowledge and belief. In M. Faller, S. Kaufmann, and M. Pauly, eds., *Formalizing the Dynamics of Information*, vol. 91 of *CSLI Lecture Notes*, pages 27–50. CSLI Publications.

Carnap, Rudolf. 1928. *Der Logische Aufbau der Welt*. Berlin: Weltkreis-Verlag. (Translated by R. A. George as *The Logical Structure of the World*, (London: Routledge & Kegan Paul, 1967).).

Carnap, Rudolf. 1937. *The Logical Syntax of Language*. London: Routledge & Kegan Paul. Translated by Amethe Smeaton (Countess von Zeppelin).

Carnap, Rudolf. 1939. *Foundations of Logic and Mathematics*, vol. 1.3 of *International Encyclopedia of Unified Science*. Chicago: Universtiy of Chicago Press.

Carnap, Rudolf. 1955. Meaning and Synonymy in Natural Languages. *Phil. Studies* 7:33–47. Reprinted in *Meaning and Necessity, Second edition*.

Carnap, Rudolf. 1963. Intellectual Autobiography. In P. A. Schilpp, ed., *The Philosophy of Rudolf Carnap*, vol. 11 of *The Library of Living Philosophers*. La Salle, Illinois: Open Court.

Carroll, Lewis. 1977. *Lewis Carroll's Symbolic Logic*. New York: Clarkson N. Potter. Edited by W. W. Bartley, III.

Chellas, Brian F. 1980. *Modal Logic: An Introduction*. Cambridge: Cambridge University Press.

Cheney, Dorothy L. and Robert M. Seyfarth. 1990. *How Monkeys See the World*. University of Chicago Press.

Cherniak, Christopher. 1986. *Minimal Rationality*. Cambridge, Mass.: MIT Press/Bradford Books.

Clark, Herbert H. and Catherine R. Marshall. 1981. Definite Reference and Mutual Knowledge. In Joshi, Webber, and Sag, eds., *Elements of Discourse Understanding*. Cambridge: Cambridge University Press.

Dummett, Michael. 1973. The justification of deduction. *Proceedings of the British Acadamy* 59:201–232. Also appears in *Truth and Other Enigmas*, Harvard University Press, 1978.

Dummett, Michael. 1991. *The Logical Basis of Metaphysics*. Harvard University Press.

Dunn, J. Michael and Gary Hardegree. 2001. *Algebraic Methods in Philosophical Logic*. Oxford University Press.

Eberle, Rolf. 1974. A Logic of Believing, Knowing, and Inferring. *Synthese* 26:356–382.

Fagin, Ronald and Joseph Y. Halpern. 1985. Belief Awareness and Limited Reasoning: Preliminary Report. In *Proceedings of the Ninth International Joint Conference on Artificial Intelligence, vol. 1*, pages 491–501. Los Altos, California: William Kaufmann Inc.

Fagin, Ronald and Joseph Y. Halpern. 1988. Belief Awareness and Limited Reasoning. *Artificial Intelligence* 34:39–76. This issue actually came out in December 1987, though the article is labelled with '1988'. A preliminary version of this article was published as [FH85].

Fagin, Ronald, Joseph Y. Halpern, Yoram Moses, and Moshe Vardi. 1995. *Reasoning About Knowledge*. MIT Press.

Fagin, Ronald, Joseph Y. Halpern, and Moshe Vardi. 1990. What is an Inference Rule? Research Report RJ 7865, IBM Research Division.

Gärdenfors, Peter. 1988. *Knowledge in Flux: Modeling the Dynamics of Epistemic States*. Cambridge, Mass.: MIT Press.

Garson, James W. 1984. Quantification in Modal Logic. In D. Gabbay and F. Guenthner, eds., *Handbook of Philosophical Logic, vol. II: Extensions of Classical Logic*, vol. 165 of *Synthese Library*, chap. II.5, pages 249–307. D. Reidel.

Geanakopolos, John. 1992. Common Knowledge. In *Theoretical Aspects of Reasoning about Knowledge: Proceedings of the Fourth Conference*, pages 254–315. San Mateo, California: Morgan Kaufmann.

Gettier, Edmund. 1963. Is justified true belief knowledge? *Analysis* 23:121–123.

Giannoni, Carlo B. 1971. *Conventionalism in Logic*. The Hague: Mouton.

Ginsberg, Matthew L., ed. 1987. *Readings in Nonmonotonic Reasoning*. Los Altos, Calif.: Morgan Kaufmann.

Goldwasser, S., S. Micali, and C. Rackoff. 1985. The Knowledge Complexity of Interactive Proof Systems. In *Proceedings of the Seventeenth Annual ACM Symposium on the Theory of Computing*, pages 291–304. New York: ACM Press.

Gray, J. N. 1978. Notes On Data Base Operating Systems. In R. Bayer, R. Graham, and G. Seegmüller, eds., *Operating Systems: An Advanced Course*, vol. 60 of *Lecture Notes in Computer Science*, chap. 3.F, pages 393–481. Springer-Verlag.

Halpern, Joseph Y. 1987. Using Reasoning About Knowledge to Analyze Distributed Systems. In J. Traub, B. Grosz, B. Lampson, and N. Nilson, eds., *Annual Review of Computer Science, Vol. 2*, pages 37–68. Palo Alto: Annual Reviews, Inc.

Halpern, Joseph Y. and Yoram Moses. 1990. Knowledge and Common Knowledge in a Distributed Environment. *Journal of the ACM* 37(3):549–587.

Halpern, Joseph Y. and Yoram Moses. 1992. A guide to the completeness and complexity for modal logics of knowledge and belief. *Artificial Intelligence* 54(3):319–379.

Halpern, Joseph Y. and Moshe Y. Vardi. 1986. The Complexity of Reasoning about Knowledge and Time: Extended Abstract. In *Proceedings of the Eighteenth Annual ACM Symposium on the Theory of Computing*, pages 304–315. New York: ACM Press.

Harman, Gilbert. 1977. Review of Jonathan Bennett's *Linguistic Behavior*. *Language* 53(2):417–424.

Hintikka, Jaakko. 1962. *Knowledge and Belief: An Introduction to the Logic of Two Notions*. Ithaca, N.Y.: Cornell University Press.

Hughes, G.E. and M.J. Cresswell. 1968. *An Introduction to Modal Logic*. London: Methuen and Co.

Kneale, William and Martha Kneale. 1962, 1984. *The Development of Logic*. Oxford: Oxford University Press.

Levesque, Hector J. 1985. A Logic of Implicit and Explicit Belief. In *AAAI–84, Proceedings of the Conference on Artificial Intelligence*, pages 198–202. Los Altos, California: William Kaufmann Inc.

Levesque, Hector J. 1990. All I Know: A Study in Artificial Intelligence. *Artificial Intelligence* 42:263–309.

Lewis, David. 1969. *Convention: A Philosophical Study*. Cambridge, Mass.: Harvard University Press.

Lismont, Luc and Philippe Mongin. 1994. A non-minimal but very weak axiomatization of common belief. *Artificial Intelligence* 70:363–374.

Lismont, Luc and Philippe Mongin. 2000. Strong completeness theorems for weak logics of common belief. Cahier 2000-352, Laboratoire d'Économétrie de l'École Polytechnique.

Luce, R. Duncan and Howard Raiffa. 1957. *Games and Decisions*. New York: John Wiley & Sons.

Maynard Smith, J. 1982. *Evolution and the Theory of Games*. Cambridge: Cambridge University Press.

Maynard Smith, John and G.R. Price. 1973. The logic of animal conflicts. *Nature* 246:15–18.

McCarthy, J., J. Sato, M. Igarashi, and T. Hayashi. 1977. On the Model Theory of Knowledge. In *IJCAI-77*. Cambridge, Mass.: MIT Press.

Menezes, Alfred C., Paul C. van Oorschot, and Scott A. Vanstone. 1997. *Handbook of Applied Cryptography*. CRC Press.

Moser, Paul K., ed. 1986. *Empirical Knowledge: Readings in Contemporary Epistemology*. Rowman & Littlefield.

Moses, Yoram. 1988. Resource-bounded Knowledge. In *Proceedings of the Second Conference on Theoretical Aspects of Reasoning about Knowledge*, pages 261–275. Los Altos, California: Morgan Kaufmann.

Moses, Yoram and Gal Nachum. 1990. Agreeing to Disagree After All (Extended Abstract). In *Theoretical Aspects of Reasoning about Knowledge: Proceedings of the Third Conference*, pages 151–168. San Mateo, California: Morgan Kaufmann.

Nash, J. F. 1951. Non-cooperative Games. *Annals of Mathematics* 54:286–295.

Nash, J. F. 1953. Two-person Cooperative Games. *Econometrica* 21:128–140.

Osborne, Martin J. and Ariel Rubinstein. 1994. *A Course in Game Theory*. MIT Press.

Pearce, David G. 1984. Rationalizable Strategic Behavior and the Problem of Perfection. *Econometrica* 52(4):1029–1050.

References / 153

Putnam, Hilary. 1983. Convention: A Theme in Philosophy. In *Realism and Reason: Philosophical Papers Vol. 3*, chap. 10, pages 170–183. Cambridge: Cambridge University Press.

Quine, Willard V. 1936. Truth by Convention. In O. H. Lee, ed., *Philosophical Essays for A. N. Whitehead*. New York: Longmans. All references to this paper herein are to its appearance in *The Ways of Paradox and other essays* by W. V. Quine (Harvard University Press, 1976).

Quine, Willard V. 1970. *Philosophy of Logic*. Englewood Cliffs, N.J.: Prentice-Hall.

Quine, Willard V. 1985. *The Time of My Life: An Autobiography*. Cambridge, Mass.: MIT Press.

Samuelson, Larry. 1988. Evolutionary Foundations of Solution Concepts for Finite, Two-Player, Normal-Form Games. In *Proceedings of the Second Conference on Theoretical Aspects of Reasoning about Knowledge*, pages 211–225. Los Altos, California: Morgan Kaufmann.

Samuelson, Larry. 1997. *Evolutionary Games and Equilibrium Selection*. MIT Press.

Schelling, Thomas C. 1960. *The Strategy of Conflict*. Cambridge, Mass.: Harvard University Press.

Selten, Reinhard. 1988. Reexamination of the Perfectness Concept for Equilibrium Points in Extensive Games. In R. Selten, ed., *Models of Strategic Rationality*, chap. 1, pages 1–31. Kluwer Academic Publishers.

Skyrms, Brian. 2000. Evolution of inference. In T. Kohler and G. Gumerman, eds., *Dynamics in Human and Primate Societies*, pages 77–88. Oxford University Press.

Stalnaker, Robert. 1994. On the evaluations of solution concepts. *Theory and Decision* 37:49–74.

Stalnaker, Robert. 1996. Knowledge, belief and counterfactual reasoning in games. *Economics and Philosophy* 12:133–163.

Stuart, Harborne W., Jr. 1997. Common belief of rationality in the finitely repeated prisoners' dilemma. *Games and Economic Behaviour* 19:133–143.

Syverson, Paul and Iliano Cervesato. 2001. The logic of authentication protocols. In R. Focardi and R. Gorrieri, eds., *Foundations of Security Analysis and Design: Tutorial Lectures, LNCS Vol. 2171*, pages 63–136. Springer-Verlag.

Syverson, Paul F. 1990. A Logic for the Analysis of Cryptographic Protocols. Formal Report 9305, NRL.

Tan, T.C. and S. Werlang. 1988a. A Guide to Knowledge and Games. In *Proceedings of the Second Conference on Theoretical Aspects of Reasoning about Knowledge*, pages 163–177. Los Altos, California: Morgan Kaufmann.

Tan, T.C. and S. Werlang. 1988b. The Bayesian Foundations of Solution Concepts of Games. *Journal of Economic Theory* 45(2):370–391.

Thomas, L. C. 1984. *Games, Theory and Application*. Chichester, England: Ellis Horwood Limited.

Tuttle, Mark. 1990. Knowledge and Distributed Computation. Technical Report 477, MIT Laboratory for Computer Science. (This report is Tuttle's 1989 dissertation from MIT.).

van Emde Boas, Peter, Jeroen Groenendijk, and Martin Stokhof. 1981. The Conway Paradox: Its Solution in an Epistemic Framework. In Groenendijk, Janssen, and Stokhof, eds., *Formal Methods in the Study of Language, Part 1*. Amsterdam: Mathematical Center.

Vardi, Moshe Y. 1989. On the Complexity of Epistemic Reasoning. In *Proceedings of the Fourth Annual Symposium on Logic in Computer Science*, pages 243–252. Washington, D.C.: IEEE Computer Society Press.

von Neumann, John. 1937. Über ein ökonomisches Gleichingsystem und eine Vereallgemeinering des Brouwererschen Fixpunktsetzes. In K. Menger, ed., *Ergebnisse eines Math. Coll.*, **8**, pages 73–83.

von Neumann, John and Oskar Morgenstern. 1944. *Theory of Games and Economic Behavior*. Princeton, New Jersey: Princeton University Press.

Wäneryd, Karl. 1993. Cheap talk, coordination, and evolutionary stability. *Games and Economic Behavior* 5:532–546.

Index

Abadi, M., 92
accessibility relation, 75–77
Anderson, A.R., 147
Aristotle, 1, 142
assignment function, 79
Aumann, R., 53, 134, 135
authentication, 60–62, 99
awareness, 9, 97, 100–119
awareness function, 104–109, 117
axiom
   awareness axioms, 109–110, 118
   familiarity axioms, 81–82
   knowledge (**T**), 51, 52
   negative introspection (**5**), 51, 75, 97
   positive introspection (**4**), 77, 97

Barcan, R., *see* Carnap-Barcan Formula
Barcan Formula, *see* Carnap-Barcan Formula
Barwise, J., 39–40, 42–44, 49, 54, 68, 70–72, 75, 91, 97, 117, 119
belief, *see* knowledge
Belnap, N., 147
Bencivenga, E., 75, 78
Bernheim, B.D., 134
Bicchieri, C., 134
Black, M., 5, 6, 65
Bonanno, G., 53, 60

Carnap, R., 1–4, 7, 103

Carnap-Barcan Formula, 77, 88–89
Carroll, L., 5
Cervesato, I., 61
Chellas, B., 51, 77, 84, 99
Cheney, D., 139–141
Cherniak, C., 136
Clark, H., 43, 60
co-induction, 54, 68–69, 71, 117–118
common knowledge, 39–44
   bottom-up view of, 54
   finite representation of, 42–43
   in convention, 53, 57, 61–63
   mutual belief and, 49–63
   operator, 96–98, 119
   top-down view of, 53–54
   vs. shared information, 70–72
common knowledge operator, 117
convention, 11, 16, 17, 28–35, 61–63
   Lewis on, 11, 14, 17, 28–35
   nonmonotonic, 130–131
   of logic, *see* conventionalism
   vs. habit, 123–130
conventionalism, 1–10, 133–148
   Carnap's, 2, 4, 7, 145
   of logic vs. mathematics, 6
   as-ifism, 7–8, 121–123
   explicit, 5, 7–8, 121–123
Conway, J., 40
coordinated attack, 44–47, 52,

56–62, 65–71, 138
  solution, 46–47, 66–67
  unsolvability, 45–46
coordination equilibrium, *see*
  equilibrium, coordination
coordination problem, 11, 17–25,
  124, 134
  solution, 21–25
Creswell, M.J., 78, 88
cryptography, 58–59, 99
  hash chain, 58–59

deduction theorem, 87
designator
  nonrigid, 92–94
disjunctive syllogism, 147
domain, 77–79, 88, 92–93, 98–99,
  101–102, 104–105, 107–109
Dummett, M., 146
Dunn, J.M., 79, 147

Eberle, R., 99
epistemic logic, *see* logic,
  epistemic
equilibrium, 14–19, 21, 23,
  134–136, 138
  coordination, 18, 19, 124, 133,
    137
  proper coordination, 20–22, 24,
    29–30, 32–33
  Nash, 134
Everett, A., 146
evolution, 134–136

Fagin, R., 3, 41, 51, 70, 72, 99,
  100, 102
familiarity, 9, 73
fixed-point, 42–43

game, 12
  cooperative, 13, 16
  evolutionary, 135
  mutual-dependence, 13
  n-person, 12
  non-cooperative, 16, 17
  nonzero-sum, 13, 16
  outcome, 12

  solution, 15
  strategy, 12, 27–35
    evolutionarily stable, 138
    optimal, 15, 16
    pure vs. mixed, 14
    alternative, 34–35
  two-person, 12
  value of, 15
  zero-sum, 13
Garson, J., 75, 81
Geanakopolos, J., 134
generals paradox, *see*
  coordinated attack
Gettier, E., 56–58
Giannoni, C., 1, 5
Goldwasser, S., 99
Gray, J.N., 44
Groenendijk, J., 40

Halpern, J., 3, 41, 42, 44–46, 51,
  65–67, 69, 70, 72, 97, 99, 100,
  102
Hardegree, G., 79
Harman, G., 42, 43, 97
Hayashi, T., 42
heap, *see* sorites paradox
Henkin, L., 84, 113
Hintikka, J., 51, 73–77, 91–92
Hughes, G.E., 78, 88
Hume, D., 63, 126

identity, *see* term
Igarashi, M., 42
indiscernibility relation, *see*
  accessibility relation
induction, 45–46, 65–69, 71
information
  vs. knowledge, 70–72
interpretation, 79

Kneale, W. and M., 1
knowledge
  belief vs., 49, 51, 52, 110
  defeasible, 67
  justified belief and, 56–58
  of situations, 94–96, 116–119

knowledge operator, 74, 95–98, 116–119
knowledge predicate, 74, 76–78, 91–95, 98–99

Levesque, H., 99
Lewis, C.I., 51
Lewis, D., 18, 20–24, 37–39, 41, 43, 49–52, 54, 62–63, 68, 122–126, 129–130
Lindenbaum, A., 84, 113
Lismont, L., 53
logic
  of knowledge, see logic, epistemic
  constructive, 142–144
  conventions of, see conventionalism
  deviant, 142–144
  epistemic, 9–10, 41, 50–54, 73–119
  free, 75, 78, 82, 108
  intuitionistic, 142–144
  of awareness
    completeness, 113–116, 118–119
    soundness, 111–113, 118–119
  of familiarity
    completeness, 84–87
    soundness, 83–84
  quantum, 142
  relevance, 142, 147
logical omniscience, 9, 53, 99–100
Luce, R.D., 12

Marshall, C., 43, 60
Maynard-Smith, J., 135, 138
McCarthy, J., 42
Menezes, .A, 58
Meyer, R., 147
Micali, S., 99
modality
  epistemic, 99–102
  epistemic vs. alethic, 76, 88–89, 92–93, 101, 110–111, 119

familiarity vs. knowledge, 98–99
Mongin, P., 53
Morgenstern, O., 12, 13
Moser, P., 53, 56
Moses, Y., 3, 41, 42, 44–46, 51, 65–67, 69, 70, 72, 97, 99, 134
mutual belief, see common knowledge
mutual expectation, 27–28, 37–39, 41
mutual knowledge, see common knowledge
mutual understanding, see common knowledge

Nachum, G., 134
Nash, J., 16, 134, 138
  Nash's Theorem, 16, 17
Nehring, K., 53, 60

Occham, 1
Osborne, M., 12

Pearce, D., 134
Perry, J., 75
possible world, see world
Price, G., 138
Putnam, H., 7–8

quantification
  existential import, 77–78
  modality and, 77, 81, 87–89
Quine, W., 1, 4–8, 11, 101, 121–123, 133, 134, 138–139, 141–147

Rackoff, C., 99
Raiffa, H., 12
regularity, 31–34
rigid designator, see designator, nonrigid
Rubinstein, A., 12

Samuelson, L., 135, 136
Sato, J., 42
Schelling, T., 11, 13

Selten, R., 134
semantic consequence, 82–83
Seyfarth, R., 139–141
shared information, *see*
    common knowledge
signaling system, 137–141
situation, 9–10, 44, 75, 103
    epistemic, 70–72, 100–102,
        110–111
    knowledge of, *see*
        knowledge, of situations
    nonmonotonic, 130–131
    shared, 39, 43–47, 49–52, 55–56
    vague shared, 69–72
Skyrms, B., 139–141
sorites paradox, 46, 65–67, 128
Stalnaker, R., 53
Stokhof, M., 40
strategy, *see* game
Stuart, H., 53
Syverson, P., 61, 73

Tan, T., 134, 135
term
    denoting vs. nondenoting,
        77–78, 101, 104–105
Thomas, L., 12, 135
Tuttle, M., 72

utility, 12

vagueness, 65–67, 69–72
    intrinsic, 66
valid, 82–83
    weakly, 112
valuation, 79
van Emde Boas, P., 40
Vanstone, S., 58
van Oorschot, P., 58
Vardi, M., 41, 51, 70, 72, 99
von Neumann, J., 12–14

Wäneryd, K., 138
Werlang, S., 134, 135
world
    epistemic, 9, 76–77, 104, 108

possible, 9–10, 44, 75, 103
    alethic, 9